KT-549-551

PENGUIN LIFE

A Mindfulness Guide for the FRAZZLED

'Witty and accessible'
Woman & Home

'If the idea of mindfulness has always seemed a bit wishy-washy, you'll be pleased to know Ruby Wax once felt the same way. Now the comedienne has written a guide to mindfulness that is a sensible way to cope with stress'
Yours

'Ruby Wax shows how and why change is a good thing'
Woman's Way

'This gem of a read will point you towards a more contented way of life . . . her passion and dedication to mental health are evident in every page'
Lady

'Ruby Wax offers her own witty and accessible take on how mindfulness really can, in her view, change lives for the

9030 00005 3733 8

ABOUT THE AUTHOR

Ruby Wax is a comedian and TV writer who also holds a Master's degree in Mindfulness-based Cognitive Therapy from Oxford University. She is the author of *Sane New World* and was recently awarded an OBE for services to mental health.

A Mindfulness Guide for the
FRAZZLED

Ruby Wax

PENGUIN LIFE

AN IMPRINT OF

PENGUIN BOOKS

PENGUIN LIFE

UK | USA | Canada | Ireland | Australia
India | New Zealand | South Africa

Penguin Books is part of the Penguin Random House group of companies
whose addresses can be found at global.penguinrandomhouse.com

LONDON BOROUGH OF WANDSWORTH	
9030 00005 3733 8	
Askews & Holts	09-Feb-2017
158.1	£8.99
	WW16020776

Brain scan image on page 73 courtesy of
Dr Paul Mullins and Professor Oliver Turnbull

All other illustrations and photographs author's own

Set in 10.93/13.76 pt Dante MT Std
Typeset by Jouve (UK), Milton Keynes
Printed in Great Britain by Clays Ltd, St Ives plc

A CIP catalogue record for this book is available from the British Library

ISBN: 978-0-241-97206-9

www.greenpenguin.co.uk

MIX
Paper from
responsible sources
FSC
www.fsc.org   FSC® C018179

Penguin Random House is committed to a
sustainable future for our business, our readers
and our planet. This book is made from Forest
Stewardship Council® certified paper.

I'd like to thank Maddy, Max and Marina Bye,
Mark Williams and me.

Oh, and my husband, Ed, though I wanted to
just keep it with 'Ms'.

And also my editor, Joanna Bowen
(but that really ruins the idea).

Contents

Looked on favourably by the Dalai Lama.

Foreword

Who am I?

For those of you who have absolutely no idea of who I am, here's a short synopsis of my life so far . . .

I'm not one for blaming my parents for my depression (the nature/ nurture argument is ongoing), but here is a little background on them which may show I didn't have a chance. Both of them escaped Austria in a bit of a rush: had they not stepped on it fast, I wouldn't be writing this now because I wouldn't exist; you'd be reading blank pages. Luckily, I come from a long line of Jewish people who spent their lives fleeing one country for the next, carrying our grandmothers and our coffee tables on our backs. The minute we set up camp somewhere, we'd have to flee again. I've inherited this syndrome of always moving on, searching for safety; trying, but never managing, to find home.

Once my parents hit those American shores, my father set up a sausage-casing empire and became known as the Casing King of Chicago. He was feared by all, especially those who were farm animals of the pork variety. Without going into too much detail, casings are made from pig intestines and encompass the blended-together bits of animal to make up a sausage. I was all set to inherit his empire, but politely declined.

My mother had a fear of dirt and spent most of her life on her knees chasing dustballs. Her method of child-rearing was based on Grimm's Fairy Tales, in which children are cooked in a pie for not washing their hands before dinner, after having had their thumbs snipped off for good measure. For more details on my parents, such as how my mother used to hunt down crumbs across enormous land masses, I point you to my first book, *How Do You Want Me?*

My parents neither spared the rod nor spoiled the child. Whenever I was punished, I secretly made a list of how much money I would charge them for each mental assault. The bill was enormous. I was never reimbursed, but they did send me to summer camp, and paid to have my teeth straightened. I thought that was nice of them, so I reduced the debt.

I was happy for two months each summer, learning the spirit of competition, from tossing a javelin to the extreme sport of canoeing. We were told, if we were losing, not to be afraid to use a handgun. It was called Camp Agawak, which probably means 'go for the jugular' in Native American; and the message was: Beat the opposition at all costs. Conquer! Conquer! Conquer!

Meanwhile, in high school I was the class joke and was, charmingly, called 'Tusks', as my front teeth resembled those of a wildebeest. I had to wear braces for ten years to move them back into the same time zone as the rest of me. Needless to say, I was not an attractive child. Yes, I know it's hard to believe, looking at me now.

As far as becoming a performer was concerned, I was not an instant success. In high school I was cast as 'Earthworm' in *Hello, Dolly!*. (It was not a big role.) But, with absolutely no experience or talent in my pocket, I moved to London, completely deluded, to become a great classical actress. I lived in a bedsit for the first ten years. The decor made it look like someone had haemorrhaged in there, and there was no heating, so I had to straddle my hairdryer to survive the frozen winters. I auditioned for every drama school but failed to get a place, despite the fact that I did a brilliant (in my mind) Juliet in a cardboard wimple that I made myself. (Never wear one: it's impossible to walk through a doorway without ripping your neck off.)

Jump cut . . . I ended up, through sheer drive, getting into the Royal Shakespeare Company; through sheer drive, I made a career in television that lasted twenty-five years; through sheer drive, I married and created a family . . . and I drove myself so hard with that same sheer drive that, seven years ago, I crashed, burned and drove off the cliffs of sanity. Shortly thereafter, I was institutionalized and sat on a chair for months, too terrified to get up. I had suffered depression all my life, but this episode was the Big Kahuna.

My 'aha' moment came when I realized I had used my success as armour to cover the chaos inside me. I'd created a fabrication, like those smiling cardboard cut-outs of showgirls in Vegas. I was just a front; and, behind the front, no one was at home. I have noticed that celebrity is a fantastic antidote to a dysfunctional early life. However, after this deepest of deep depressions, I thought I'd cut the cord of show business and move on, which was smart, because I was, in any case, becoming less popular. (I knew things were slipping when I found myself cutting a red ribbon to open a Costa at Heathrow. Terminal Three.)

I thought it would be a good time to reinvent myself and, while I was at it, find out who, exactly, had been inhabiting my brain all those years. Jump cut, again . . . I started to study mindfulness-based cognitive therapy. I never do anything by half, so I did it at Oxford University and got my

Masters, too – and before I forget, did I mention I was awarded an OBE this year? So maybe it was worth all the agony . . . but probably not.

A Mindfulness Guide for the FRAZZLED

'What does she mean by this title?' 'Why has she picked this topic?' 'How much do you think she's being paid for writing this book?' 'Do you think anyone will buy it?' 'How old is she saying she is now?' 'I never liked her TV shows.'

These are just some of the comments I've overheard from people who read my last book, *Sane New World*. Let me answer the first question: what *do* I mean by the title?

A neurobiologist might say that someone is 'stuck in a state of "frazzle".' They mean that, for this person, constant stress is overloading their nervous system, flooding it with cortisol and adrenaline; their attention is fixed on what's worrying them and not the job in hand, which can lead to burn-out. (I swear I didn't know that 'frazzled' was a technical word when I came up with the title of this book, so I must be incredibly smart and intuitive.)

Second question: why did I pick this topic? Well, I have spent most of my waking hours (and some of the sleeping ones) in the Land of Frazzledom, so I feel qualified to act as an expert tourist guide, pointing out some of the more notable swamplands of confusion and self-doubt. Take comfort in knowing that you are not alone in these lands. I've come to the conclusion that we're all in this together: many reside in the Land of Frazzledom, and we're all trying to find some kind of exit route. I've also decided that, rather than spending our time complaining, or pointing our finger at problems outside in the world for making us feel so unhinged, we need to learn to navigate those sharp rocks of uncertainty and bewilderment. In this book, I'll give you some recommendations for the best holiday destinations to rest and refuel.

PERSONAL STORY

It's November, I'm in the Ritz Hotel, London, and my mind is in a kind of haze; a thick, grey fog. I'm not sure what brought me to this event, or even how I got here. I ask what charity it's in aid of. A large, moustachioed woman in a cat-hair cardigan tells me: 'Save the puffin'. She happens to be the spokesperson for the charity and later gives a moving speech, in that 'wee' Scottish brogue, about how difficult it is for puffins to land on the rocks in the Orkneys because of the strong winds, and that once they *have* managed to land and lay their (one) egg, they have big problems stopping it blowing away. No mention of global warming, just that the birds can't land there any more.

The world is melting down, and I'm listening to someone talking about how hard puffins have it. I have to restrain myself from shouting, *Why don't you just ship them all to Miami? End of problem.*

Every three to five years, this fog would come down and I would have a spell of depression . . . but they didn't have a name for it back then. It was called 'having a turn' – or a 'whoopsie', as my parents liked to call it. So, for example, they would say my mother was having a 'whoopsie' when she was cleaning the ceiling with a wet wipe. I could never tell when I'd flipped, but a big clue was that I'd end up at events like the Save the Puffin one I've just described above. I probably kept up a frenzy of activity to show the world and myself that nothing was wrong with me and that my behaviour was perfectly normal. I was trying to disguise the fact that I had lost my mind. It was like putting a plaster over a tumour.

Another time, shortly after the puffin event that November, I found myself about to do a scuba dive under Brighton Pier as part of my diver's licence. I was frozen blue, my teeth were clanging, weights were being added to my belt . . . and then I dropped in a straight line to thirty feet below and found myself looking at a shopping trolley and a flip-flop. Where were the reefs? The parrotfish? It seemed to me that other people got those things in their life, but all I got was a trolley and a flip-flop . . .

Now, a little background on how I came to study mindfulness-based cognitive therapy. The only reason – and, I repeat, *the only reason* – I went for it was because of the impressive scientific evidence proving that it has the highest success rate in treating a whole pot-pourri of physical and mental disorders.

I chose to study it because I had been taken to the cleaners by every psychological intervention known to man (and woman), from plain vanilla therapy (where I talked about how nuts my parents were for so long I turned it into a one-woman show) to alternative therapeutic bizarreties such as hitting a pillow with a bat for three days while calling it Daddy, then giving it a funeral, burying it and mourning it. I'm ashamed to say I did do a session of rebirthing, where they stuck me in a bathtub with a snorkel and, afterwards, pulled me out by my heels. (It was just as bad as the first time around.) Don't get me going, but I also went to a person who wore medieval attire and said she channelled Merlin yet spoke in her own San Diego accent, albeit with some 'thou's and 'm'lud's thrown in. Her husband, in jerkin, tights, and octopus hat with jester bells, served mead. (I could go on, but it's for another book.) Call me crazy, but after all this, I decided that science was the best way forward.

So, after my last bout of depression seven years ago, I promised myself I'd learn to somehow lasso my wild mind and take some action. Obsessed, I plunged into research mode, scouring science journals and papers. Here's what I found. With depression alone, for those who've had three or more episodes, mindfulness-based cognitive therapy yields a 60 per cent chance of preventing relapse. What really hooked me was the fact that you do it on your own: no running to shrinks shouting, 'Fix me!' at all hours . . . and the best news of all is: it's free (being a Jew, for me that's half the cure). Initially, I thought that 'mindfulness' meant sitting erect on a hillock, your legs in a knot, humming a mantra that was probably the phone book sung backwards. But I was still prepared to give it a whirl.

Let me make it clear that I take medication for my depression, just as you would for any other physical illness. However, if antidepressants carried a guarantee, no one would ever relapse, and yet most of us do . . . many times. This is why I've added meditation to my medication. Think of it as wearing two condoms: double protection.

I hope I'm not sounding too evangelical; mindfulness works for me, but each one of us has a different fingerprint and you should follow whatever works for you. If you want to crawl to Lourdes and smooch Our Lady's feet and it makes you feel better, go for it.

Anyway, I happened to have recently received my Masters in mindfulness-based cognitive therapy from Oxford. (Can I please start calling it MBCT? It gets tiring spelling it all out the whole time.) So that's why this book is about MBCT.

What's between the Covers?

Chapter 1: Why FRAZZLED? All this evolution, and we're still not perfect. Even though we're up on all twos, can miraculously balance on seven-inch heels and have the largest brain of all in the animal kingdom, we're still half cooked.

This chapter is about us, and why our wisdom isn't up to speed.

Chapter 2: Mindfulness: Who? What? Why? What is this thing called mindfulness, and why would we need it? What, in our own brains, is keeping us from that elusive concept 'happiness'?

Chapter 3: How Our Brains Work and the Science behind Mindfulness In this chapter, I show off how smart I am, giving neurological evidence as to why MBCT is so effective when dealing with stress. By stress, I don't mean you had a bad-hair day, I mean the stress that eventually helps to shorten your life.

Chapter 4: A Depressing Interlude I had a bit of a depression after writing Chapter 3, so, after a long gap, I wrote Chapter 4 . . . It will all make sense when you read it.

Chapter 5: The Six-week Mindfulness Course MBCT is normally taught in an eight-week training course. After that, it's up to you to practise what you have learnt. It's no longer about running to someone and asking them to help patch up your broken psyche; now *you* are in charge. I'll provide an easy and amusing six-week MBCT course. (In case you're worried, my interpretation of the course has been approved by my professor at Oxford, Mark Williams, a co-founder of the discipline of MBCT; I didn't just make it up last night and think, 'What the hell, who's going to find out?')

Chapter 6: The Social Mind: Mindful Relationships This chapter is all about using mindfulness to improve relationships with friends, family, community, country and the world. We only survive and flourish because of others, so I'd say that skilful bonding is probably the number-one skill to go for. Basically, this chapter contains my top tips on empathy.

Chapter 7: Mindfulness for Parents, Babies and Children In this chapter I will offer some mindfulness exercises for parents to use with their children, and for parents to use on themselves. (Before we even get to the kids, we have to fix the parents. If they aren't aware of their own issues, their kids don't stand a chance.)

Chapter 8: Mindfulness for Older Kids and Teenagers If you try to give any advice to your teen, you'll be as effective as an irritating, buzzing mosquito that just won't die. The only way they'll deign even to think about the benefits of being able to focus their mind and lower their stress level is if they suss that it'll help them to deal with peer pressure, exam pressure and every other pressure that breaks out during that hailstorm of hormones. I'm also including a bit about mindfulness in schools: the successful and widely used .b (dot b) programme.

Chapter 9: Mindfulness and Me In this chapter I'll be putting my money where my mind is by having my brain scanned before and after an intensive silent retreat which involves seven hours of mindfulness practice a day. I'll be keeping a journal throughout my silence . . . unless they take my pen away.

Appendices A couple of scientific bits to back me up.

. . . and finally, some Notes from a Madwoman: Throughout this book I'll be dropping in snippets of personal stories. When I do this, you'll know, because it will look **like this**.

1

Why FRAZZLED?

We are all frazzled, *all* of us . . . well, most of us . . . well, some of my friends are. When I say 'us', I'm referring to the 'us' in the free world who live relatively scot-free of invasion, hunger, plague and the raining-down of frogs; the lucky 'us' who've won the jackpot by being born in the right place at the right time. And yet we, the winners, complain of stress. Why can't we enjoy the fact we can live to 109 and still keep our own teeth? We should be popping the champagne cork for the simple fact we're breathing. I, too, am guilty of creating stress where there doesn't need to be any. While I'm writing this book, I'm incredibly stressed: paranoid that I'm spelting everything''s rite. I should be stressed when a bomb is about to drop on my head, not because I don't know where, commas, go ir indeed ani punktuation? It's the thinking about stress that stresses us out, not the incidents themselves.

When I say that we are in a state of emergency, I don't mean the terror, both real and imagined, that lurks, about an impending Third World War triggered by anyone from the nut-job who runs North Korea to the endless other nut-jobs in charge of their countries. No, the emergency I'm talking about is that unless we wake soon from our sleep-walking state, we're on a downhill slide of our own making; in terms of evolution – emotionally, anyway – we're heading back to being on all fours. We have sent rockets into space to explore the cosmos but have for some reason neglected to explore ourselves. We just keep trying to achieve and compete, with absolutely no insight as to why. We need to set an alarm clock to shake ourselves out of this stupor, to get us out of the mindset where we brood and worry, and bring ourselves, literally, to our senses. That's the only way to experience life: not through words, but through sight, smell, sound, touch, taste . . . how many forkfuls have you shoved into your mouth today and actually tasted? I don't know when, historically, we fell asleep at the wheel, because we definitely began our existence awake; as primitive beings, we were awake to the sound of every cracking twig and every twitching bush. Now, however, we just tunnel our way through life on autopilot, as fast as we can, to get our stuff done and neatly put away in drawers.

We should be struggling to evolve towards living a peaceful life, not just finishing the next chore on the list, believing that, when it's done, *then* we'll start living. No more postponement: it's getting late in the day. Either we learn how to wake up now or we sleepwalk into death.

The Evolution of Our Brains

Like it or not, we all started as a tiny individual cell. In order to understand who we are today, we need to give a nod to our protoplasmic past. It wasn't even all that long ago when we began; only for the last 200,000 years have we been truly modern, erect humans; before that we were fish, lizards and an assortment of apes. (Not the most sophisticated of lineages.) Most of us are hopelessly unaware of the extent to which we're held hostage by our moronic beginnings.

In some ways, we've achieved a lot (i.e. being able to make devilled eggs), but as far as our emotional development is concerned we're still swimming with the pond scum. My opinion is that we need to take into consideration the influence of our roots in our prehistoric past. We can pretend to be civilized, with our teas and our scones, but, underneath, the primitive still beats its drum.

The very first thing to develop, and something we share with other mammals, is a brain that ensures survival. This means that we, like other mammals, are always on the lookout for danger. There's this endless search for happiness, but let me ruin your day by telling you that we are in fact natural-born pessimists because, that way, we keep the species going. We have to be ready for danger. This is why we have a leaning to the negative rather than the rosy. Someone once said that for every five negative thoughts we have only one positive one. But in this culture it's not the unexpected meteorite that's going to nix us but things like deadlines and mortgage repayments; you can't run away from the national deficit.

The problem is that we're unaware that part of our brains still plays by the rules of 500 million years ago. I'm talking about the 'kill and mate' school of thought. As evolved as we think we are, we're still cave folk with Stone Age brains, but now we're trying to deal with the complexities of the twenty-first century. This could be the reason why we need so many shrinks and so much medication.

In the beginning, things were fine: we lived in tribes with our family members. We all shared the same genes, so we trusted and protected each other. The bad thing about that is the bit about all being related to each other, which caused infinite mutations; some of our cousins had more fingers than they needed, others had feet that grew backwards. The problems began when tribes started to expand, cities grew up and civilization developed. Then we had to make rules to control our deeper, darker desires, i.e. don't sleep with your sister. Freud tried to help us rein in our ids, but our baser, primordial selves are still sliming around under the surface. Repression doesn't help; that savage inside is always lurking, ready to let it rip.

The Evolution of Stress

Earlier in our existence, life was tough, but no one died of stress. They died of disease. They died because of old age (around twenty-two and a half), accidents, childbirth, bad teeth . . . but not from stress.

There was no word for stress, so no one complained about it.

My theory is that the concept of stress kicked in only when we came up with language. We could no longer just sling a spear, now we had thoughts with words that gave us internal reviews of how well or badly we flung it. Usually, they were bad.

Don't get me wrong: a lot of good has come out of thinking. I'm thinking right now and probably you are, too, so that's good. But with this new consciousness came stress.

Then the floodgates opened because we needed more space in our brains to fit in all that thinking, so around 100,000 years ago (I can't give you an exact date), out of the blue, we found that our brains had grown about three times bigger in size. It could have been the weather, or a tilt of the planet, but we had a big mental-growth spurt. Probably the reason we had to get up on all twos was to keep all that grey matter balanced on our necks. As soon as we had our extra-large brain, we started to wonder what we could fill it with. One great thing about the leap in brain size was that we could stop grovelling in the mud like our cousin the ape and begin to invent things, like bubble wrap. Stress came with these great inventions because we had to repair them, insure them and change their batteries; no one was going to do it for us, certainly not our ape friends (who are still of no use, except to amuse us with what they can do with a banana).

Our big brains pushed us to conquer new frontiers; we filled up the Earth with shopping centres and nail bars, but then what? So we became pioneers of thought, using technology instead of the Conestoga wagon to raise our flag in new and far-off lands, hurtling out our opinions, political stances, our likes and dislikes, no longer on foot but through the Internet.

We were lulled into thinking that, with the dawn of computers (thanks, Bill G.), they would do all the boring stuff and allow us to chase butterflies or flower-arrange. It turns out we're now stuck with doing the boring stuff, while the computers are having the time of their lives: hacking into the World Bank, giving Stephen Hawking an American accent. I predict that we'll eventually be so redundant that we'll all be replaced and devolve into a technological accessory.

The Crammed Brain

No one is addressing the exhausted elephant in the room: why are we making our lives more difficult? Why do we stuff ourselves full of so much detritus? We put all that garbage in there – why can't we just scoop it out again? There's not going to be some test at the end of our lives, so why are we cramming so much? I know *I'm* at my limit. I've had to send my memory to the cloud now, and I don't know how to get it back down again.

Zillions of bits of information downloading into computers with more processing power than Apollo mission control are coursing up to your brain through your fingertips. David Levitan writes, 'Today, just to communicate with friends, not counting work, each of us produces on average 100,000 words every day, there are 21,274 TV stations and it will take 17 lifetimes, if you live to be 158 in each life, to get through all the channels on your TV' – and most of them are crap. We take in all that information at a cost; it's exhausting to try to figure out what we need and what is trivia. We're so clogged up upstairs it's difficult to make sensible decisions: should I worry about Iceland defrosting or about getting the right toothpaste? Our brains are not computers, they don't need charging; they need to rest, and there is no rest. Who has time to rest? . . . It's become a dirty word. The only time you can legitimately rest is when you're in the restroom. Every tweet, Facebook entry and text is sucking out your energy. That's why you always forget where you parked your car.

While we complain that our 'to do' lists are endless, let us not forget that we begat those lists; no one from outer space came when we weren't looking and implanted 'the list' in our brains. Okay, let's say we really do need to jot down a few things of importance, like needing to buy milk or to have a colonoscopy, but when that 'things that must be done' list goes into the hundreds per day, we should be concerned. Maybe we keep adding new things in the fear that, if we ever got through our list, we'd have no purpose, no reason to take another step. If you were suddenly list-less, would you just grind to a halt? What happens when that happens? Even though everyone complains about how much stuff they have to do, what would they do if they had nothing to do? 'To do or not to do, that is the question.' People who haven't got a single open three-minute slot in their day because they're dashing from meetings to lunches to workouts to appointments to cocktails are thought of in our society as great achievers, they are role models, but in my opinion (and I say this with compassion) they should be burnt at the stake for making many of us feel inadequate.

Other creatures know what they're doing. Birds, for example, migrate thousands of miles to lay an egg and then fly all the way back to where they came from for more random sex; no one complains. We, who don't have to swim, fly or canter a thousand miles, are dropping from exhaustion for no other reason than that we are trying to keep up with the next guy . . . who's keeping up with the next guy, who's heading toward a full nervous breakdown. To be human is to stand up and claim your weakness. If you do that, others around you will feel compassion and empathy (little-used qualities), and that's how the world will recover from its diseases of greed and narcissism.

We need to wake up and notice the signals that our minds and bodies are giving us; to slow down sometimes and notice the scenery. I don't mean for ever, just to stop for petrol once in a while before going back to the race we call life. I know a neuroscientist who recently had a severe heart attack. You'd think he'd know something about brains. He'd know that they don't run for ever on two hours' sleep and 400 hours of work a week. He announced after only three days that he was not going to take a single day off work and would resume his lectures from his hospital bed, plugged into a lung machine and nasal feeding tubes, thus proving that neuroscientists can also be idiots.

Comparison

Another thing that is frazzling us is that we constantly compare ourselves to other people, always sniffing around to find out who's top gun. In the natural world, a female honeybee larva can grow up to be either a queen or a worker, depending on what food it's fed. Hives are complex social structures with different kinds of workers, such as harvesters, nurses and cleaners; there are no footballer-wife bees or celebrity bees. Everyone gets fed and there is no competition; the cleaner bee wouldn't dream of being a nurse bee. We, however, feel we need to do it all: be the queen, lay the eggs, clean, breed, and learn to hula-hoop at the same time. This is why we end up on Xanax and bees don't. Anyway, I know about comparison: it's one of the ingredients of my neurotic soup.

I'm in Edinburgh feeling miserable, and I'm trying to figure out why. On the surface, everything is running smoothly – my show, my life, my work – so what's wrong? I finally come up with a reason.

I am at a dinner, sitting next to Brian Cox. I am sick to my stomach because he is a molecular geneticist, astrophysicist, seeker, particle physicalist, quantum-electro-hydro-collidist.

He's beautiful and looks ten years old. This is hitting one of my triggers: comparison. I try to pull out something from the empty space called my brain, giving it my best shot. I say, tongue sticking to the roof of my mouth, 'If there are infinite parallel universes, which means that there are zillions of "me"s, how am I able to put food in my mouth with one fork?'

Maybe he thinks I have a point, so he continues telling me that 600,000 years ago, when there was finally enough oxygen, a cell filled with mitochondria (I nod as if I know what this is) from some piece of fungus started to breathe in oxygen, while another cell breathed out methane. I have no cards to play. I think I might pretend to faint.

The gap of silence grows too long, and he refocuses, on to a guy across from us, and tells him that scientists can determine how far a cell can migrate from central Africa to Egypt. The guy doesn't respond, so I'm thinking he's as stupid as me, but then Brian tells me he's the world's leading cosmologist. I shrivel. Carlos Frenk (look him up on You-Tube; I did and almost choked to death). The evening doesn't end well. I might have drunk too much. No one asked for my phone number.

It's that old chestnut 'comparison' that drives us mad. Some people are satisfied with their lot – I know they're out there in the country somewhere, among the trees, growing their own chickens, pulling udders for a living and sitting around the fire roasting marshmallows. As for the rest of us, we're assaulted by messages from the ether, about what we don't have but should have if we want to be cool. It's no longer just about keeping up with your neighbour but about leaving that neighbour in the dust, seething with resentment.

Comparison goes way back. 'Why isn't my cave dress as nice as Fran's?' 'Why don't I have a bigger codpiece?' It's always the same – 'Why? Why? Why?' – and that's what makes us stressed. We strive, we strive, and we strive some more. It's always been the way: we suffer from conceits and illusions that tear us apart; we're like hungry ghosts, always seeking, wanting, yearning for something. Soon there will be epitaphs that read: 'She died of envy' or 'He croaked because his car was too small.'

The title of my theme song is 'Never Good Enough'. When I'm with the highly brainy, I turn into my thirteen-year-old moron self. I'm suddenly in the back of the class, useless and gormless, with my protruding teeth. The longer I'm with these people, the less able I become to articulate anything, which makes me feel that I'm even lower down the ladder of intelligence. I usually try to keep them talking so they don't find out that I know nothing.

I recently asked Lord, Professor, Dr, surgeon and all-round genius Robert Winston to have tea with me. He has honorary doctorates from sixteen universities; I have half a one. When I was in a particularly cocky mood, after he'd seen my show at the Hay Festival and complimented me on it, I asked, and he agreed and suggested we meet at the House of Lords. On the day itself I started to panic, wondering what exactly I was going to talk to him about.

Okay: jump cut. I'm sitting with Lord R. in one of those holy of holies, a wood-panelled room lined with oil paintings of old politicians, and I'm being served tea by bowing men in tuxedos. It is at that point I realize I have nothing to say. I ask Lord R. what he is up to, and he graciously tells me about his worldwide research on epigenetics. I've heard of epigenetics, but it's not my specialty, to say the least. I'm now sweating, and my stomach has left the building; I'm going to have a seizure if he asks me anything about anything. I'm thinking of going into the loo and Googling 'epigenetics' so he'll like me and not think I'm brain-damaged. I don't remember much after that, except trying to be funny (that's a card I throw to lure in the opposition), but when I try too hard to be funny it always backfires badly. It's an act of sheer desperation.

On our way out, we grind to a halt and stand frozen while some guy in a red suit with gold buttons walks down the *Addams Family* hallway carrying a gold septum (I know that's not right, but I don't know how to spell the word for that gold baton someone really important uses to beat on the floor before a session is about to start in chambers . . . or whatever).

Once he passes and we move on, Lord R. introduces me to other lords and ladies; I made small curtsies and bows in a below-stairs-servant, *Downton Abbey* kind of way. I am introduced to a Lady Somebody, who, I am told, changed the divorce laws in the UK. She is obviously brilliant, and again I lose my ability to speak a single word of English. We move on, and I say to a passing lord (who I happen to have met before), 'I'm not worthy.' When he's about twenty feet past me he shouts back, 'Yes, you are.' That got me out of the building without wetting myself in shame. Life is full of small miracles.

Choice

Here's another fly, or bee, in the ointment of why we're so . . . antsy all the time: choice. When I came to the UK, I would have killed for ice cream that wasn't strawberry or vanilla. Even then, the US was making thirty-one flavours; now it's 1,310. It started slowly – chocolate, mint, bubblegum, bacon with egg, alfalfa, no calories, no fat . . . no ice cream. Now, the UK has not only caught up but has overtaken the US. Choice is ruining our lives, taking up precious moments.

I'd say that 99 per cent of our lives is now taken up by the act of deciding (and not just about ice cream). We suffer from decision overload: we forget we have a limit, and if we push it too much we hit neural fatigue. We should have stuck with vanilla.

Some of the above 'frazzlers' are contemporary problems that come with our Western culture whether we like it or not, but there are certain evolutionary human features we're born with; they've worked brilliantly for us in the past but are now backfiring down the street of life like an old banger.

Autopilot

A great feature of the human brain is that we're able to string together numerous actions and bung them all into one activity. You don't have to think: pick up toothbrush, open cap, squeeze tube, grimace, move toothbrush up then down, then up again and down again, then spit. Each separate action would take up a big chunk of your lifetime.

Thanks to human mutations, cruise control enables us to perform without our needing to use conscious thought. This is the benefit of being on autopilot: being able to daisy-chain all those separate actions into one. The flip side of this gift, however, is that, because we're creatures of habit, we end up staying in automatic gear and not noticing anything around us. Before we know it, our whole life begins to be a series of events all clumped together and so we end up missing the ride. Holidays, weddings, Christmas, the day you lose your virginity (though it wasn't the most pleasant experience for me and is better forgotten) – all are done on automatic, to get them over with so we can move on to the next mission.

Most of the time we need to watch a video to remember any sort of occasion.

I'm aware how much of my life I've lived on autopilot, spending my days elbowing my way through a career and worrying, whenever I got what I wanted, that someone would take it away and so elbowing some more. I can't recall much of a normal life outside of pushing. I sometimes meet men who tell me we once dated, and I have no recollection of it. Where was my mind? Perhaps they laced my drink with some date-rape drug.

You won't recognize you're on autopilot when you're on it because that's the point of it: to not think, just do.

When Autopilot is Useful

- On a long train ride through Siberia with people sitting on your head it's so crowded
- When you have to go shopping with your mother
- When you have to watch a school play your kid's not in
- When you're plucking a chicken (I haven't, but I've heard)
- Being at Glastonbury and needing to go to the toilet
- Being a dinner guest in Japan and your host is serving pufferfish (not to be confused with puffin). It can kill you

When Autopilot isn't Useful

- During sex (sometimes)
- When you're eating in a Michelin five-star restaurant
- On any holiday with your children
- When you're tightrope walking

Multitasking

If we were anatomically equipped to deal with the require-ments of the twenty-first century, we'd have 476 hands, 75 ears, 451 mouths and 16 orifices. Multitasking is another fabulous ability humans have that animals don't. No other animal comes with the ability to spin so many plates. Have you ever seen a gazelle listening to headphones, tweeting and smoking a joint at the same time? I don't think so. We pride ourselves on our ability to multitask, boasting about how many activ-ities we can cram into a second, and yet it's not only what keeps us from being in the present but also what burns us out.

When our computers overload we know to switch them off and boot them up again a bit later. Why can't we do that to ourselves without feeling like a failure? I'm not suggesting we all 'chill' (God I hate that word and all who use it), but if we could just know to put our fingers to sleep after an orgy of emailing so that we can concentrate on the cheeseburger we've just ordered, life would be a bowl of chips to go with it.

Past and Future Thinking

I've said this before, but just to remind you: stress and a high level of vigilance worked for us in the past because we had to figure out quickly what was safe and what wasn't. If there was a rustling in the bushes, was it something with big teeth looking for lunch or was it a friend playing a prank? (If so, it wasn't funny.) You need to imagine the past in order to pre-dict the future outcome.

This ability to time travel enables us to stay on Earth another day. Many animals do this, recalling what's dangerous and what isn't, but they don't worry about it. Obviously, a mouse recalls that an elephant will kill it and, faced with another one, knows to run away. But the mouse doesn't worry about it, it doesn't stay up all night fretting that it might happen, it just skedaddles off. The mouse has it sussed. We don't.

The fact is our memories give us very unreliable feedback of what really happened during any incident and, each time we recall it, the images get fuzzier and fuzzier. So when we go back to our memory files we're working from some pretty shoddy evidence. This means that past and future thinking is taking up our valuable airtime and energy, and to very little advantage.

When Past and Future Thinking is Helpful

- Oh, I remember, this is the man who tried to mug me last month; maybe I should cross the street
- Oh, this is where the hole in the pavement was that I fell into and broke my skull; maybe I should walk around it

When Past and Future Thinking isn't Helpful

- I ate a really bad snail when I was nine so if I see anything that looks like a snail I have to kill it, even if it's a hat that looks like a snail
- I reported a man who was wearing a badly fitting toupee for sexual harassment. Now whenever I see someone with a bad toupee I scream, 'Rapist!' and run away

Past and future thinking causes us endless angst because we're constantly caught in a trap of remembering so many imagined disasters that no longer have anything to do with survival and this leads to rumination; one negative, self-focused thought snowballs into the next, into infinity. 'Why did I flunk the exam?' 'Why didn't I get the job/ the boy-friend/ girlfriend? Probably because I'm a loser. If only I was smarter/ had a better personality/ was better-looking . . . I'll probably never amount to much because I'm too stupid/ ugly/ overweight . . . Was I born this way? Can I get surgery? . . .' (It never ends.)

You'll never know why you feel the way you feel; thinking will never get to the bottom of your thoughts. These negative thoughts feed negative feelings, and the cycle of despair deepens. Operating like this is like taking poison to kill the poison. That theory of ingesting something toxic to fight something toxic might work with homeopathy, but it doesn't when you apply stress to stress. When we scramble for an explanation, whatever we come up with is usually wrong, because we've only got a few thousand words and over 50,000 feelings. It's like trying to speak Spanish when you only know the word 'tapas'.

The human brain – specifically, Einstein's – can come up with the equation $e = mc^2$ (that's how smart we are), but what our mind can't do is come up with the solution to something like 'Why don't people I have sex with ever call me again?' Even Einstein probably couldn't answer that one.

Being on automatic pilot, multitasking and using past or future thinking are all techniques for ensuring survival, but they can also be at the heart of our unhappiness. (In the next chapter, on mindfulness, I'll discuss how all three can be revamped and made to work for us, rather than against us.)

Loneliness

Why, if there are 7 billion people on Earth, do I feel so alone? I do so much with my fingers to keep in touch with people that I've forgotten that what I really need to do is get up and go somewhere to meet them. I sometimes get a wake-up call and think that I haven't spoken with my mouth or seen the flesh of a real friend for twelve years. I panic that I might be forgotten because I haven't spoken to someone so I send a vague message, but I don't know how to write something from the heart, something personal, because I've only been using my computer to order things online. I know how to order a Danish superior goosedown-filled duvet and I'm quite proud of that talent, but how to say, 'I miss you,' without typing an emoticon of a stupid grinning circle and a pumping heart is beyond me. I'm now so used to using these things I put a heart and a kiss symbol on emails to my bank manager and my plumber.

This is the problem: all this interconnectedness and we still feel lonely; and the less we feel the need to emotionally connect with each other, the more we'll lose our ability to. You can spend the rest of your life online but it will never make you feel the same way as when someone covered in skin smiles at you. We might just have lost that human touch of togetherness because sending a smiley face doesn't say it all.

We use our phones now to feel connected. You see people pincered between headphones, laughing, screaming and crying, with full arm-waving gestures, into a plastic rectangle. They're probably talking to their iWife or iHusband, complaining about something that's happened in their iHome.

Recently, I was in Ireland and went to the tiny town of Westport, where everyone acts like you're a long-lost relative and is thrilled to welcome you, giving you a 'Top o' the morning' greeting even when it's not morning. They talk about having a 'crack', which I didn't get until I left. (I thought they were on the stuff.) And just when I was thinking the town is so provincial, and I was getting snotty, they take me to a pub: and there is the reason we should all live in Ireland.

In the corner of the dark, smoky, wooden-floored pub are several fiddlers, three flautists, a singer and someone banging a drum. They're playing that Irish music that makes your heart bleed; it all sounds the same, but it's fantastic. One guy from the Chieftains (a brilliant Irish band) was playing along with them and I was told this music goes on most every night. Everyone in there was dancing – old, young, totally plastered – and everyone was completely happy. I was thinking how much we're missing out on in London. Here, the whole community gets together and they have these evenings like they're one big family. I was told that when someone dies in the town everyone piles into the house of the bereaved and they take care of the cooking and cleaning, and there's music and crying and drinking. How much would I love to live there in my next life!

The Search for Happiness

This is what we're all after, but one of the problems with the 'H' word is that we can't agree on what it is and how you hold on to it.

We share all our other emotions because we all come with the same equipment. When you bang your elbow on something hard, even if you're a member of some isolated Amazonian tribe the response is 'Owww!' (but in Amazonian). Sadness is fairly universal, too: the reasons for it change, but we all get the same sensation of water dripping out of our tear ducts and our chins wobbling.

Happiness is the big banana we're all after, and yet we

have no idea why or how the other guy feels it. There are not many books written about the feeling of what actually happens when you bang your elbow, but there are billions on happiness.

What is known is that, if you make it through a life-or-death situation, you get that feeling of feathers tickling your insides and the sides of your mouth turn up into a smile.

The situations below may create a feeling of happiness.

- You just crossed the Himalayas with no food for two weeks and suddenly see a rabbit
- After fifty years of searching, you found your birth mother . . . and she's rich
- You've just been told the diagnosis was wrong: you haven't got something terminal
- You were blind and now you can see, and you live in Barbados

Some of these experiences may be more the 'R' word, as in 'relief', rather than full on the 'H' word, but let's not get caught up in semantics; you get a big *zing!* if you've experienced any of the above.

If you are in an emergency situation, happiness is more elusive. I'd just like to remind you that I realize I'm only addressing about 5 per cent of the people in the world in this book: those who have enough food in their mouths, and clothes on their backs. Most people on this globe don't have the time to contemplate happiness; whether they live or die is just a flip of a coin. I apologize to them – not that they'd be reading this book, but if they happen to be using some of the pages to build a fire and read any of this . . . I'm sorry.

Some big names have talked about happiness, and they're no dummies.

Seneca: 'The only thing we own is our mind, everything else is a gift.'

Epicurus said that there are only three important ingredients to happiness: friendship, freedom (not to be owned by anyone), and an analysed life. The more you lack these three things, the more you'll want power and money, and they always lead to unhappiness.

Aristotle wrote that happiness is the goal of goals.

Nietzsche wrote that great happiness requires great suffering.

Dr Seuss: 'Don't cry because it's over; smile because it happened.'

Kurt Vonnegut: 'I urge you to please notice when you are happy and exclaim or even murmur or think at some point, "If this isn't nice, I don't know what is."'

Abraham Lincoln: 'Most folks are as happy as they make up their minds to be.'

Buddha: 'Life is suffering.' (I love that guy.)

Unknown Person: 'If you think sunshine brings you happiness, then you haven't danced in the rain.' (This person has clearly never had depression.)

Dalai Lama XIV: 'Happiness is not something ready made. It comes from your actions.'

Basically, all these people agree with me . . .

Okay: here's my stance on happiness.

We all (well, I do) get a volt of joy when we're selected for the girls' volleyball team (I wasn't, but I can imagine the thrill if I had been . . . Clearly, I'm still very bitter) or fall in love . . . when the feeling's mutual (which didn't happen much in my early life, so I took up stalking).

The rub is that, however high the hit is, it doesn't last; none of us can keep up that emotional erection for ever. Even if you hold on to the second feeling long enough to marry, some day you'll eventually look at him/ her and think, 'What was I thinking?' The day will come when you'll be sitting there, hating the way he/ she chews food. Everything ends. However talented, beautiful, intelligent you are, at some point you will be replaced, like an old toaster, by a newer model. So there it is: we spend our lives hunting for something that has a very limited shelf life, sometimes lasting only seconds. If orgasms went on for ever, we'd never get anything done.

Contentment

If we can't even describe happiness accurately, we really have a hard time with contentment. It sounds like you've retired and are smiling benignly in your incontinence pants. It sounds like that, but it isn't. The problem is we have to *learn* to feel contentment. I know that when I've done something for someone else without expecting anything in return I get a warm, syrupy feeling in my veins. That's how I would describe how contentment feels, but it only works if you do your altruistic act in private, and don't shout it out from the treetops. If I announce, 'Hey, everyone, I helped save a puffin,' it wouldn't feel as good as secretly saving a puffin . . . (I might be losing my thread here . . .)

I think my aim in life is to try for that state when you're

not too high or too low, to just be able to balance on the surfboard. 'You can't stop the waves, but you can learn to surf' – I read that on a T-shirt. This brings me back to why I practise mindfulness each and every day: to stay on that surfboard.

The Future of Humanity

As far as our evolutionary advancements are concerned, we don't need any more thumbs in order to survive, or to be able to run any faster, thanks to the car industry. The way we'll advance as a species in the future will be to psychologically catch up with our technology. Please believe me: I'm not whining about there being too much technology, no one is more thrilled than I that someday I might be able to get a virtual Brazilian – but we will have to learn to recognize when we're running on empty and to pull over to rest and refuel.

I think a useful accessory would be a bleeper implanted in our brains that tells us when to pull up and stop for a breather; we won't lose out because, when we join the race again, we'll be quicker, more resilient and able to beat the competition. (Yes, you can use mindfulness to help you win the race without killing yourself in the process.)

I like it when people say, 'I screwed up. I don't know what I'm doing. I am scared. I'm lost.' To be human is to stand up and claim your weakness.

We should admire people who can just stay in bed and not worry about it. We should say, 'Wow, this guy can afford spare time, let's give him a knighthood.' In truth, when we meet someone who seems perfect, secretly, we can't wait for his or her demise. If someone is flawed, I know I am immediately drawn to them, reassured that they are like me underneath. But because we never express our limitations for fear of being ousted by the tribe, we keep quiet and hide our imperfections while feeling doused in shame. This secrecy and refusal to be open makes us feel alone and isolated.

Conclusion

The next time we evolve, it won't be at the whim of natural selection, it will be by *our* selection, and it will be a matter of consciously developing our emotional insight rather than inventing some other 'thing' that might be technologically jaw-dropping but won't make our lives any easier or happier. We have enough smarts. Now we need more hearts.

I've noticed that when people are extremely successful they start to believe they're invincible. They're so busy being smart they forget they're just a piece of meat with a sell-by date; they don't even have a flicker of awareness about their own mortality. They forget that they, too, are biodegradable and must be handled with care, or they can kiss themselves bye-bye.

If we don't develop our more human qualities then we're doomed, evolution-wise, to become cyborgs, our cells replaced by silicon chips, steel pincers for fingers (but hundreds of them to do all the multitasking), and then we'll be perfect, no flaws, only a shiny, silver carcass with an imprint of an Apple where our hearts used to be.

2

Mindfulness: Who? What? Why?

Don't just do something, sit there.

First, What It Isn't

Before I start, I'd like to give you my personal list of what I think mindfulness isn't.

1. Learning to be nice to people
2. Saying hello to your dishes before you wash them, or learning to love your soap before you wash with it
3. Standing naked in the rain and smiling inanely
4. Moving in slow motion so that everyone behind you gets into a pile-up
5. Becoming nothingness while sitting in your underwear
6. Seeing God and/ or Santa
7. A one-way ticket to nirvana or Burning Man (same thing)
8. Leaving your old skin behind and becoming a part of everything, only thinner

What It Is

Mindfulness is a way of exercising your ability to pay attention: when you can bring focus to something, the critical thoughts quieten down. We're told, especially as children, to pay attention, but we have no instructions on how exactly to go about it. Go on: train your attention on something or someone and try to keep it there. You might for a few seconds, but after that it will flit away on to the next thing like a butterfly on heat. You probably won't even notice you're now focusing on something else because you weren't paying attention in the first place. It's not about paying attention to something *outside* but about being able to focus *inside*, being able to stand back and watch your thoughts without the usual commentary on them. As with any skill that has to be developed, you have to practise; it isn't part of the human package. My definition of mindfulness is noticing your thoughts and feelings without kicking your own ass while you're doing it.

I think of the relationship we have with our own mind as being the same as a rider with their horse. Sometimes the horse (the mind) wants its freedom to gallop or eat ferns and so it rips the reins out of your hands, dragging your arms out of their sockets as it does so. To bring mindfulness in: you feel like, if you jerk on the reins, your mind will probably resist you even more, but if you gently pull back on them, making that clicking cowboy sound with your tongue, and saying, 'Whoa, boy,' gradually your mind will slow down, obey you and then you can (horse) whisper, 'Thank you.' If your mind wants to run away with you and you violently try to pull it back, it will buck you off and bolt. If you treat yourself with compassion and resist obeying your demanding thoughts, they become quiet.

When you're in observer mode, just witnessing your thoughts, they lose their power and sting as you begin to realize that you aren't your thoughts. If thoughts were who you are, how would you be able to observe them?

When you're purely watching, you're circumnavigating words, thoughts, concepts and judgements. If you hold back your impulse to act on your thoughts, you'll eventually notice that they keep moving, coming and going of their own volition; some heavy, some light, some adorable, some pornographic. All you have to do is sit back, kick off your shoes and watch that TV show called *You* without getting dragged into the story.

Mindfulness strengthens your inner observer, giving you an awareness of your own thought processes, as if you're sitting above your thoughts, watching. It's not dissimilar to when you're watching yourself in a dream and you know you're dreaming.

It sounds easy, but it's not; your mind is desperate to snatch you back. It's had you at its beck and call for twenty, thirty, ninety (however old you are) years; it's not giving up that easily.

Think of your mind as a laboratory, and you're investigating what's on the table without having any preconceptions or making any judgement on it. Does a scientist have an attitude when they're looking at a fly's eyeball in the microscope? No.

Acceptance

When you use mindfulness, you learn to accept things the way they are without trying to change them. It is the gateway to the 'shit happens' school of enlightenment. Everyone wants things to be better, but they mostly aren't, so what are you going to do about it? Have a hissy fit? This is a hard one to swallow, but swallow it you must if you want to go to sleep at night. As the observer, you witness the good, the bad and the ugly without giving a running commentary on whether you like what you're seeing or not. Once you start doing that, you've lost your seat on the sidelines and will be sucked back into the crossfire of words.

Here's a little metaphor to help you understand your thoughts. Picture your mind as a bottle of clear water with sand at the bottom. When it's agitated by thoughts or feelings, it's as if you've shaken the bottle: the sand disperses and the water is now murky. When you hold the bottle still, the sand settles, just as your mind settles when you watch thoughts rather than reacting to them. As I said, you can't *think* your way out of an emotional problem; the effort it takes to find out why you feel the way you feel always makes things worse. It's like being trapped in quicksand: the more you struggle to get out of it, the deeper you sink. You have to accept that you can't stop the thoughts, but you can stop what happens next.

If we run away from our shadows they will follow us, but if we run toward them they will run away. (I'm sure someone once said that.)

For those of you who've tried to study mindfulness but found having to look into your own mind – especially when it's a pigsty – too torturing or boring to do every day, I understand completely. The problem is, even if you aren't aware of the toxic thoughts in your head, they're still there. You can run, you can hide, you can wish them away, but they remain. You may believe you're having a hunky-dory time, with the perfect kids/ wife/ teeth but, someday, if you don't look into the darkness in the basement of your brain, it will erupt spewing lava everywhere. If you don't deal with it, you'll keep slinging your mess over everyone else and blaming them for creating yours.

I have this lifelong mantra: 'Who can I blame?' If there's

something I don't like about me, I will find an unassuming person, pin my crap on them then give them hell and whip them like an old, defunct mule. I'm extremely accomplished at pointing my finger at someone for making me furious rather than U-turning the telescope on to myself to see who is actually the culprit. I don't think I'm alone when I say that I treat everyone around me the way I treat myself. We project the stuff in our minds not just on to our family and friends but on to the whole planet. I assume everyone's out to get me because I'm probably out to get them. We are the real enemy to ourselves; everyone else is decoration.

You can't learn mindfulness by taking a pill (I, who love pills, only wish you could); nor can you thrust yourself upon a reiki master/ dog whisperer/ juicer every time you feel your mind declaring war. No one can help you except you, and only you. The big yawn about this is that, as with any other skill, you have to practise it in order to break old habits. It's the only way you'll be able to get off cruise control and start to notice the scenery, smell the roses, taste the chocolate and hear the cry of a she-wolf.

It takes gallons of willpower for you to get yourself to sit and practise but, to be honest, I don't love lugging myself into the shower every day either. (Sometimes I skip it; don't tell anyone.) Even when I'm brushing my teeth, I'm not having the time of my life. Look on the discipline of sitting and practising each day as a personal achievement, as I do . . . after giving myself every excuse known to man for not doing it: my house is on fire, I have to find my missing sock immediately . . . especially if the house is on fire.

Every morning I hoick myself up on to a chair to practise mindfulness, and it's torture, having to listen to the

maelstrom of madness in my head. It feels like someone's switched on a gigantic leaf-blower and is scattering my already insanely scattered thoughts. I'm usually berating myself to get up and do something important rather than sit there like a doorstop. Each morning begins with a list that goes to infinity and beyond of things I have to do, not just that day, but for the rest of my life. There's not much of a tune, but here are the lyrics . . .

Glue chipped soap-dish, defrost turkey, think about Ebola, find phone, email everyone about something, re-shellac shellacked nail, write this book, check lump on cat . . . I could understand if I had something really important to think about, like I needed heart surgery, but to think about re-shellacking my nails is unforgivable. Those are the things I have to do . . . but some things are impossible, like call Kim Jong-un the North Korea guy and tell him to pull himself together. I have lost more than half my life immersed in these lists. They continue no matter what I'm doing, when I'm on stage, during sex . . . they never stop: Why didn't my mother let me get a real Christmas tree? I should get a fake one. My bra had those foam cups in it: where did I leave them? I will never forgive Dagmar Stewart for stealing my Barbie's cocktail dress when I was eight. I want bratwurst with mustard. When did I last go snowboarding? Did I dream it or was I really in a plane crash in Bavaria, or Fort Lauderdale, when it landed in whipped cream? I have to buy shampoo, I hate my feet, is it too late to join the Royal Ballet, was I an orphan?

So why do I stay on the chair if I have to listen to all this horror?

Sometimes I'll only notice one inhale or a few exhales during the whole twenty minutes of sitting before the usual soundtrack – Get up, you idiot, and order a bathmat – starts blasting. But each time I manage to pull my attention away from the distractions and back to the breath, it feels as if I'm holding on to a flag pole in order not to blow away during a raging storm. Sometimes I can actually sit back and watch the storm upstairs, as if I'm watching a TV show, and even if the show is awful, the lines are awful and the characters (usually just me) are awful, I do get some distance. It's so much less painful when I feel as if I'm *watching* a horrible situation rather than being in one. And this is what gets me up on the chair each day, knowing that this muscle that pulls me back from the fray is getting stronger every time I go from the anxious thoughts to a breath. Mindfulness is the only thing I know to do that can dig me out of despair and give me even a few moments' break from my brain.

Training That Brain

If you're thinking, 'I still can't do it' as in 'You can't teach an old dog new tricks' (you being the dog), I ask you to answer these questions: Did you come out of the womb knowing how to slam-dunk a basketball? Did you automatically know how to speak Swahili? Cook a barbecue? Pole dance?

No, you did not. Everything you do except excrete, eat and breathe, you have to learn by rote. We need to exercise what's in our heads just like we do any other muscle. Why is there so much resistance when it comes to mental exercise?

There are very few of us who enjoy going to the gym and doing endless repetitions of sit-ups. This is a waste of a life, if anything is. You want health? Take a walk. When I came to the UK thirty years ago, people weren't even brushing their teeth; now they're in the gym every day of the week, pumping.

It is rare for me to go to the gym nowadays, because if I see other people doing fifty sit-ups, I have to do a hundred with a 5kg hat on my head. I'm mindful that I have this Rottweiler gene that kicks in when I'm among other people; even if they're top athletes, a part of me wants to grab the pole and vault higher. I can't even watch the Olympics – I would destroy myself trying to hurdle the coffee table.

This is one characteristic I could really hate myself for, but since practising mindfulness, I recognize that this is part of who I am and I have begun weaning myself off self-flagellation. Now when I exercise in a class I keep my eyes shut and just focus in on my body.

Compassion: Hold the Punishment

For me, one of the hardest parts of practising mindfulness is getting to grips with self-compassion, which is the bedrock of mindfulness.

I don't even like discussing the 'C' word, because it's the last thing you want to give yourself when you're thinking negatively. You're furious at yourself for being sad or anxious when you have everything and can order a takeaway Swedish meatball at four o'clock in the morning while other people are fighting for their lives in war zones. The last thing you think you deserve is kindness. Also, when I hear of people being kind to themselves, I picture the types who light scented candles in their bathrooms and sink into a tub of Himalayan foetal-yak milk.

When I went to study mindfulness at Oxford, I asked my

professor, Mark Williams, about my aversion to self-kindness, and he said that when I sit down and practise mindfulness, even if it's just for a minute, that alone is being kind to myself. And if you're kind to yourself, then you're in the right mind to pass that kindness on to others. Just giving myself a break from the constant list-making and self-bullying, he said, is compassion.

I know I sound nihilistic, but I do try to make peace with my pessimism. Even in childhood, my thoughts were never cuddly and warm. They were mostly unforgiving; I know no one is as cruel to me as me. I've always lobbed grenades at myself. If I try to stop, the thoughts only get more persistent. The only way I have to ease the situation is by practising mindfulness, and now I have done so for many years. When I do this I feel like I'm doing mental sit-ups, going from breath to thought, thought to breath, so that the watcher becomes easier to access. Sometimes I notice only one inhale or exhale in the twenty minutes and, just as I start to enjoy it, my mind sabotages my attention and I'm back to the usual soundtrack: *You forgot to order the bathmat, you moron.*

We all have a watcher: it's when we suddenly become aware of our thoughts or actions. 'Oh, look, I'm biting my nails,' or 'I'm tasting food rather than gorging on it.' Mindfulness is the only thing I know to do that can dig me out of despair and can give me even a few seconds of time out from me.

How to Do It

Hold your horses. In Chapter 5, I'll be giving you my six-week training course and implanting the 'how to's of mindfulness into your virgin brains. You will learn how to notice when your mind is on the rampage and bring it back to a state of calm and clarity in order to be able to make better decisions and, as a bonus, to take a trip to the present. For me, to be able to bring myself from a busy-brain state to equanimity is the most rewarding thing I can do for myself. And I think that holds true for you, too.

Just like learning any other skill that takes practice, it doesn't just come by crossing your fingers. Mindfulness exercises aren't difficult in themselves – in fact, they're often pleasurable – the hard bit is that you have to do them every day, even if it is for only a few minutes, to reap the benefits. Before you roll your eyes, let me remind you that whatever you've learnt in your life you've learnt it through repetition, including the ability to read this *word*. Eventually, you will be able to use mindfulness whenever you need it in your daily life, but first you need to build some muscle to strengthen your ability to focus.

So you begin by focusing in on what's going on in your mind. (You check the weather outside, now you're checking it inside.) If it's nice and breezy, have a great day and get on with what you're doing. If you notice high gusts of critical thinking or storms of stress moving in, intentionally move your focus to one of your senses (sight, taste, smell, hearing and touch).

The point of this is that as soon as you're focused on a sense the gabbling mind automatically becomes just background noise, because you can't be focused on a sense and thoughts at the same time. The human brain just can't do it; it's either one or the other. Focusing on the senses keeps you grounded while your thoughts jump around you. With practice, you will build your ability to shift your mind intentionally when distractions arise.

I think that becoming mindful is a result of intentionality.

Once you have made the effort to shift your focus intentionally, you're immediately in the present. You can't listen to a sound tomorrow or yesterday, it's always now, and when you're in 'the now', there are no critical thoughts, just feelings. This ability to focus on a sense works as the anchor for you and for your practice of mindfulness.

Attention

What keeps me practising mindfulness, even if I'm not in the mood (and, believe me, that's often), is the fact that I understand the impact it has on the brain and therefore on well-being. With sit-ups, you'll see the results: you'll have some ripples down your front, and that keeps you going. With mindfulness, each time you practise, you're building up an area in your brain that corresponds with your ability to pay attention. Your thinking mind will beg, scream and tantalize you, trying to drag you off wherever it wants, but if you can keep focus the benefits are biological, psychological and neurological. *Boom!* I bet you never connected all those with paying attention. If you want to be happy, learn how to pay attention.

No one describes attention as well as Dr Daniel Siegel, who combines brain science with psychotherapy and shows us how to tame the mind and create a happier and healthier life for ourselves.

He says, 'Focused attention helps us to see the internal workings of our own minds; to be aware of our mental processes without being swept away by them; to redirect our thoughts and feelings rather than being driven by them. Paying attention enables us to get off autopilot and moves us beyond the reactive emotional loops we can trap ourselves in. By developing the ability to focus our attention on our inner world, we're picking up a scalpel and resculpting our neural pathways. How we pay attention shapes the structure of our brains.'

I truly love this man Siegel. I got to talk to him once in LA. We arranged to meet at a vegetarian restaurant. I got there early and was so nervous I tried out various tables and chairs to find which would be best to meet him in. I tried to calm down and when he came in I stood up and knocked over the water glass. I then handed him his book to sign, completely soaked, the print smeared, and tried to pretend it hadn't happened.

The Golden Fleece of practising mindfulness is the skill of paying attention. I know it sounds easy but, trust me, we don't automatically know how to do it. We can only pay attention to something for, on average, about 1.2 seconds and then our eye, driven by our mind, flits to something else. Our minds aren't built to linger; we keep flitting: it's the mission statement of every cell in our bodies to keep checking our surroundings for possible danger, otherwise we wouldn't be here, we would have been on some kebab millions of years ago. Remember: our brain has no idea the caveman days are over so, God bless it, it's still vigilant for predators.

How many sunsets have I missed while staring right at them? If I see an American bald eagle or my kids doing a school play, I want to be able to tear my mind away from the soundtrack of mundanity and focus on the only thing worth watching on earth at that moment. Even my cat Sox can focus. He can stay riveted on a piece of string for days on end. So I sit there practising mindfulness each day just to do what my cat does so naturally.

To be able to shift attention at will is my solution to how we can live better, be happier and stay healthier, because it means we are now in control of this magnificent and complex pile of a trillion cells, rather than being run ragged by it.

I knew a man whom I believed was at the pinnacle of success, someone in the Fortune 500 who sat on at least fifty prestigious boards. He ended up having a heart attack, and when his wife went to visit him in the hospital she found a woman tending to him with a sponge . . . who turned out to be his other wife, who had three children. These types of people believe themselves to exist way above us pitiful mortals, and above the law. They're completely unconscious of their behaviour; living their life detached from any overview. Usually, these people are brought to their knees by their own hubris. Had this man learnt to pay attention, he would have become conscious and been aware that, someday, the two wives would meet and sue his pants off.

Attention works like a muscle – if you don't use it, you lose it – so to keep it on top form you need to practise, practise and practise again. A well-honed muscle of attention helps us to keep our eye on the button, to make the right decisions even amidst all the incoming stimuli and emotional turmoil of our lives.

In 2006 the word 'pizzled' came into existence. It's a combination of 'puzzled' and 'pissed' and is used to describe the feeling people get when someone whips out a phone mid-conversation and starts to talk to someone else. At that time, people felt upset about this type of behaviour; now, it's completely normal. What all this free-flowing digital information consumes is our attention and, ironically, it causes its decline.

If the mind can't pull itself out of endless loop tapes, we may find ourselves suffering from anxiety disorders, obsessive behaviours, depression or general helplessness. The skill of disengaging our attention from one thing and moving it to another will help you find the road to happiness.

Often, our attention isn't on anything; it's just shooting the breeze. Mind-wandering itself isn't the enemy by any means; the question really is: what is it wandering away from? If you're caught on a rumination jag, it's not useful; you're chewing over something that will never be swallowed. If, however, you're mind-wandering and moving toward a light bulb of insight, then it's a gift.

With a clearer, calmer mind you can think more creatively and productively. When your thoughts cause fear or anxiety, your mind gets clogged up and so you grab for safety and live on autopilot, deadlocked in your narrow view of the world.

This is something I read somewhere (I can't remember everything): if you repeat your thoughts, they become an action. If you repeat an action, it becomes a habit. A repeated habit creates a fixed persona. A fixed persona becomes your destiny.

When your mind is freed up you can access the many sides of you; we're much more multifaceted than we realize, which makes life richer, but unpredictable; we never know which side of our personalities will come to the fore. In certain situations I become shy and blushy; in others I'm a bulldozer, sometimes a tongue-tied teenager. With mindfulness you become more aware of which particular role you're playing in the moment and then decide if you want to play on or reconsider and change tack. Ultimately, we're the sculptor and the sculpted with regard to our brains and therefore our identities.

Actors know how to use this to their advantage. They

fill themselves with the thoughts and feelings of the character they are playing and even if they, as a person, are nervous, they will overcome it by becoming the character. I know an actor who, when you talk to him, has a terrible stammer but, on stage, he becomes Henry V: no stutter, and running England.

Who We Are

Whenever we pay attention to something, whole cascades of chemicals fire into action, while the neurons wire up to new partners in that neuronal dance that never stops. (I'll discuss this in Chapter 3.) Every millisecond, we shift our attention, and in that millisecond our brain has a complete makeover and changes shape; the mind is in a continual state of shape-shifting as we morph from one state to another.

Luckily, we come equipped with an autobiographical memory (the file we carry of all the experiences we've ever had), so it can give us pretty quick feedback on who we were yesterday and other important information such as our favourite colour, the name of our first cat, etc. If you didn't have that, you'd be like the guy in the film *Memento*, having to look at the tattoos on your arms to figure out who you slept with the night before and whether you're male or female. The autobiographical memory is the story of you so far. (Memory is not accurate but, even if the details are dubious, it's still the only life story we've got.)

Before any thought comes to our minds, our body has already reacted, either through the sympathetic or the para-sympathetic nervous system. It takes milliseconds for our minds to translate what any emotion or feeling might mean. The translation happens after the feelings have been shunted to the memory files to check if you've had a similar feeling in the past, whether it was dangerous, and what you did. It's not always accurate, because no situation is exactly the same, and your memory is not dependable: it makes things up. Ever witnessed an accident? Not only does it seem like all the witnesses were on different planets but your own report on what happened will change slightly every time you open your mouth. Sometimes you get a thought in your head that's been instigated by a feeling and you can't make a conscious connection as to why. Ever get a stabbing feeling in your stomach that makes you feel nauseous, and all you're doing is sitting in your car, backing out of a parking space? You're racking your brain, trying to figure out why you're getting this fear rush, when nothing's really going on. What might have happened is that your memory went off piste because of present associations with things from the past (your memory can't really tell time). You've flipped because your memory remembers you being in a car park when you were six and Daddy by accident left you in the car and went on holiday. So now you're sitting there in an unrelated car park at the age of fifty-seven and your teeth are chattering with fright. In actuality, when we think we know how we feel, for example, betrayed or guilty, it may just be a digestive problem or wind. Our minds try their best to come up with an explanation in spite of our dodgy memory file. It's like playing Pin the Tail on the Donkey: you're blindfolded and just guessing where to jab it in. Women will relate to this, as they know from experience that when they want to *twunk* an arrow into the head of everyone at work it might not have anything to do with what those people have done but is probably because those nasty monthly hormones are rearing their heads again. When a blues singer sings the blues about her man skipping town with her money and her mother being a hooker and her father a hog, it might just be acid reflux.

You'll never know what's really going on inside you. Even if you have a living autopsy done on yourself, no one will ever get to the bottom of 'you' . . . unless they're a proctologist.

You have various other kinds of memory, which are stored throughout your brain so you can remember how to use certain skills and know how to react to certain situations. Each time you learn or experience something new, the neurons make connections which reflect that experience and release chemicals which trigger particular feelings. It's these feelings that help you remember the experience. That is how memory is laid down. If you smell turkey and suddenly feel warm and tingly, you can go to the filing cabinet marked 'turkey smell', play the video back of Grandma stooped over the oven on Thanksgiving and relive the whole experience; all of this little mind-movie switched on by a simple smell. Get on a bicycle and your motor memory will take over, informing every part of your body of what to do. You don't ever have to consciously think about it.

So where we direct the spotlight of our attention defines who 'we' are in that second, and whatever we imagine or experience becomes a physiological reality on our neuronal map, and that is who 'we' is. Every feeling, be it fear, love, lust or hate, is expressed in our neural wiring, and therefore in the chemicals which result from these connections. If you're in Hawaii but your mind is still working late at the office, that is the place your mind resides: in the office – so you may as well still be there. Or if you're in a cinema, watching a chase scene, the wiring of your brain manifests a pattern of terror and thrills that produces rivers of adrenaline. After a minute or so you shove some popcorn into your mouth and your attention refocuses, signalling to the saliva glands to start pumping, and in this second your whole being is the essence of salt and crunchiness.

So what this all proves is that when you recognize that your mind always leans to the negative, you can learn to shift it intentionally to something more positive or fulfilling. You'll have moved to Happyville. So there you go. The next time you think attention is just an abstract concept, think again: it's as real as you are.

In the Zone

Being 'in the zone' is said to be one of the greatest feelings we experience. It's when we're in one, single-minded, pin-point focus; all other distractions fade into the background and we're working at our optimum, in the present. And, best of all, the critical voices are hushed. Bring out the confetti and the party hats.

In the zone, you feel as if you are cocooned in that complete concentration (which only lasts a limited time before you start to think about the urgency of watering that plant). All those usual niggling nags of the 'to do' list fade into the ether. I live for that sensation when, instead of feeling like an old sack humped over a computer banging out random words, I feel the computer and I are one, working together towards a common goal.

People say that being in the zone feels effortless, liberating, superhuman; you stay focused because, each time you achieve a little more success in whatever it is you're doing, your brain releases a hit of dopamine. It's that leap of joy in your heart when you splash into the pool after doing a double-back, jack-knife triple somersault off the high-dive board with both feet perfectly pointed. It's not the actual swan dive that gives you the kick, it's the hits of dopamine that give you the buzz. The swan dive actually hurts like hell.

Sometimes, writing this book, I get into that gloriously liberating zone where everything flows and I don't have to keep using the thesaurus to find the exact right word. I love that state so much I won't let go, even though I might be so tired my eyes are shutting and my mind is mush. I'm trying so hard to be aware of when I might be hitting the tipping point, when I might go from being inspired into a moron state, and end up writing gobbledegook. It's always hard for me to stop and be nice to myself, because there's still a little voice saying, 'You're so lazy! You've only worked sixteen hours! What's wrong with you?' I keep forgetting that, if I rest even for a few moments, I'm able to work better and longer and even dip back into the zone.

So with mindfulness, you become aware of awareness. This state is not to be confused with being in the zone, where you're so concentrated on a single activity you have absolutely no awareness of the outside world; you're completely lost in the task at hand. When you're in the flow, you can't be reflective and take time to notice where your mind is or to make a decision to take a break.

So if you really crave for the 'in the zone' experience, the question is: how do you keep that single-minded focus while staying aware of your inner state? I don't think you can be on both planes simultaneously, unless you've done thousands of hours of meditation, like those monks who can sing two notes at the same time (those tones that sound like they're burping). The ideal state would be to be able to be in the zone yet notice, even for a hair's breadth of a second, when it's time to pull out, to give yourself a pause to re-energize your brain, by taking a walk, a bath, watching TV, kicking a football, going out shopping or, if you're really gung-ho, doing a three-minute mindfulness exercise (see the six-week mindfulness course in Chapter 5).

The most important thing is to not bash yourself over the head when you notice your work is getting wobbly: the whole point of mindfulness is the noticing, rather than the getting it right.

Back to the Benefits of Mindfulness

I wrote in Chapter 1 about some of our human gifts, such as being able to perform on autopilot, also being a curse. Practising mindfulness is simply a way to break out of autopilot and train ourselves to do something that isn't a natural gift; we aren't born with the facility to focus, to calm ourselves and become present at will. If you can do this naturally already, put down the book, call the Dalai Lama's people and tell them you're the next one.

I hear you say, 'What about people who have minds that don't drive them at all? The ones who lie around all day on the sofa like sea slugs, watching Geordie Shore. Are these people the next Dalai Lama, too?' No. Even though they are on the sofa, they are probably not present on the sofa and their minds are ruminating as much as the obsessive home decorator or eBay addict. The liers-down, you might just find, also have a nagging voice inside telling them to get up off their ever-expanding behinds. They're probably drinking and gobbling potato chips to dull down or blank out their critical voices.

Research

Laboratory testing can measure exactly how much stronger the mind becomes with practice, and it demonstrates significant improvements over a relatively brief period of time. Dr Amish Jha has applied computer-based testing to measure the attentional performance of a group of medical and nursing students at the University of Pennsylvania, Philadelphia, before and after an eight-week mindfulness-based training course. The class taught these students to use mindfulness to manage stress, enhance their communication skills and cultivate empathy.

After the training, testing revealed that those students who were taught mindfulness could intentionally direct and focus their attention more quickly than a matched group of those who were not.

Other experiments undertaken in Dr Jha's lab have demonstrated that practising mindfulness for as little as twelve minutes a day improves the ability to resist distraction.

Being Present

An enormous benefit of mindfulness is that you get a free ticket to that rare destination: the present. Okay, I hear you say, 'What's so great about being in the present moment? What if I don't want to stare at a butterfly wing or hear the single *ting* of a wind chime? I have places to go, people to meet.'

Being present can't be understood through cognition, it's a felt experience; you feel through your senses, not through your thoughts. Simply to sit with your eyes closed and breathe probably seems like the last thing on earth you'd need, or have time, to do. You might think that by the time you've flossed your gums, done some ab crunches, taken a shower, moisturized, toasted toast, had sex with your boyfriend (notice I didn't say husband; later in life, you can skip that bit) you've used up half your day and it hasn't even started yet.

So when people speak of being mindful or present, it's usually thought of as being pretty low down in the hierarchy of needs.

On the face of it it seems that nothing is really useful about being in the present, so we don't visit it much. We don't really know how to be present except when something out of the ordinary happens, for example, your house is on fire or a seagull lands on your head. Sometimes we find ourselves having an 'aha' moment when we wake from the daydream and have a sudden insight, a revelation, when the doors of perception are thrown open for a blip in time. No one really knows how to make an 'aha' moment, but you know an 'aha' moment when you have one.

MBCT teaches you to be able to come into the present when you choose to, which is no easy feat. Try it now? See? You're all over the place, probably not even reading my book; sometimes even I'm not concentrating now, writing it: I'm looking out of the window, thinking about things like I have to call my friend Dagmar Stewart who I haven't spoken to since kindergarten . . . then suddenly I have no idea what I'm typing.

And yet the present is where everyone wants to be. If you don't believe me, let me point out that the reason you plan a holiday or an event for months in advance is to experience it 'in the moment'. But when you get to your dream hotel or tent, your mind will probably be on something else: 'Why did I spend all this money? Why didn't I go on a diet? I look like Moby Dick. I forgot to feed the hamster. This isn't as good as I thought it would be. I bet it's better someplace else.' You spend a fortune on a wine that costs more than the annual GDP of Bolivia to relish its woody undertones but your mind is somewhere else so you miss the whole experience, and now you're urinating it out without having tasted it. So much of what we do in our everyday lives is to achieve an experience, a taste, smell, sight or sound in the moment. So when people say, 'I don't really care about being present,' remind them how much money and time they're spending to get there.

If, when you're asked what's the best time of your life, you can answer, 'Now,' you've arrived.

I'm going to finish this chapter with a quote from Stephen Sutton, a teenage cancer victim who said, 'You have 86,400 seconds today. Don't waste a single one.'

3

How Our Brains Work and the Science behind Mindfulness

You may be thinking (though how would I know?) that it's all very well me going on about living in the present. I can hear you now: 'I haven't got time, I have emails to answer, mouths to feed . . . I'll get to the happiness stuff later.' I completely see your point. I, too, am in a rush, trying to finish this book to deadline and not really thinking about happiness, just on how screwed I'll be if I don't hand the book in. (Obviously, I did; otherwise you wouldn't be reading this.)

But there are many other benefits of mindfulness besides visiting the present. Current research shows that, with the practice of mindfulness, we can change the inner landscape of our brains to improve, among other things, the immune system, and resistance to depression, and to lower the risk of heart disease and enhance well-being. The research shows that it also gains positive results in helping us manage our feelings and be able to take charge.

Everyone assumes that we're pre-packaged, set in stone at birth. Not so . . . if you listen to neuroscientists (and why wouldn't you?), they will say that the brain is plastic, changing with every encounter, experience and thought. Here's what I don't understand: if something called neuroplasticity is a hard, cold fact, why haven't we, the masses, heard much about it? Why are we left sitting here with a measly fourteen shades of grey, when, if we're talking about the brain, there are a trillion possible shades.

OUR BRAINS CAN BE TRAINED TO CHANGE FOR THE BET-TER! Why isn't this in the headlines of every newspaper in the land and on breakfast TV? We can't even say now that we're stuck with the genes we were given, because recently someone has come up with something called epigenetics, a science that tells us that our genes, too, can be revamped by life experiences and environmental factors. So if you inherit some lousy genes, they don't necessarily switch on; it's like carrying a grenade throughout your life without the pin ever being pulled.

I became obsessed with neuroscience because it made me feel less alone when I realized that we all have pretty much the same equipment under our scalps. We all share the same glitches – I realize now that they aren't my fault, they're just a matter of evolution. Now when someone gives me grief, I'm aware that it might not have anything to do with me but rather that some part of their brain has flipped its lid and I just happen to be in the firing line. The fact that the brain is malleable throughout life means it's not too late for me to break some of my uglier habits of thinking. With practice, I'll be able to self-regulate, reconfigure my neural wiring and sharpen my attentional focus – just like it says on the tin.

I'm tempted to rename MBCT 'Mind Fitness'; it sounds less vegetarian. Also, it's cheaper than any gym you'll ever join, because the equipment is all in your head. The more you understand how the brain works and, using the evidence of brain imaging and MRI studies, see how much it can change, the easier it becomes to see the point of sitting down and prac-tising. So here's a little guide to what's inside your head. Before I start, I need to say that neuroscience is the most complex subject on this planet and all the universes put together. I was listening to Brian Cox and a famous neuroscientist talking on the radio, and after Brian did one of his fluty monologues about the cosmos, the neuroscientist said, 'Well, it's not rocket science. Neuroscience is much more complex.'

I asked for advice on this chapter from a very well-known neuroscientist, Professor Oliver Turnbull: neuropsychologist, Pro Vice-Chancellor (Teaching and Learning) of the School of Psychology at Bangor University and author of over 150 neuroscience publications. To help me, he gave me a few research papers to read. I can honestly say, Oliver, I didn't understand one word.

So if I said I was simplifying neuroscience here, that would be a serious understatement; it would be like Peppa Pig explaining quantum physics. I'm only going to discuss the regions, circuits and functions of the brain that are associated with self-regulation and attentional focus. Another reason for my interest is that I think neuroscientists (specifically, their minds) are the sexiest things on earth and writing this gives me an excuse to meet them.

The Three-brain Theory

I'd like to begin with the fact that none of us ever feels as if we're in our right mind. The reason may well be that we have three brains and, at any moment, we don't know which one we're in. Each brain has been shaped by evolution to improve our abilities at many tasks, from swinging on trees to getting a prenuptial. At times, each brain isn't aware of what the other two are up to.

This triple-decker reflects our evolutionary development from the earliest model (single-celled bacteria) to the latest (George Clooney). Each brain refused to be replaced by the other, each stood its ground, so they're all just crammed together in a cerebral car crash.

(Many scientists are in debate over this three-brain theory and have been for decades. Each brain isn't actually independent, they're linked, in complicated and poorly understood ways, but I'm saying they're separate to make it easier for you – and me – to follow.)

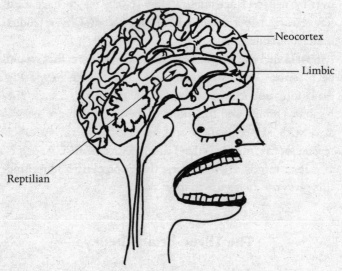

Here is my drawing. (I drew this myself.)

The Reptilian Brain

Five hundred million years or so ago we began with the oldest part of our brain, known as the reptilian brain, or archipallium (fancy name: you won't need to remember it). This very archaic area (our brain stem and the layers around and above it) is in charge of the basics: breathing, heart rate, sleep, sex and strong emotion (my type of guy).

The Limbic System

Then, 200 million or so years ago we developed the paleo-pallium, or limbic, brain, which moved in right on top and around the reptilian model and set up shop. The limbic emotionally translates the deep drives and signals from the older brain, which helps us remember our feelings, who caused them and where we were when we had them. With this later brain on the block, we also began to care for our young. Before that, we just squeezed 'em out and skedaddled.

The Neocortex

About three and a half million years ago, we (*Homo sapiens*) had a growth spurt, mostly in the cerebral hemispheres. This new, giant brain was called the neo-mammalian brain, or the neocortex; it's the big-boy brain, in charge of problem solving, self-regulation, insight, impulse control, attention, empathy . . . and, amazingly, it allows us to think about thinking.

Basically, the raw emotion shoots up from the brain stem, the limbic registers the emotions, analyses and remembers them, then the neocortex evaluates them and decides what to do next.

All Three Brains

Imagine these three brains as neighbours. Think of the conversations:

REPTILIAN BRAIN (angry): Want to f**k, grunt, eat, sleep. Duh.

NEOCORTEX: You're a despicable, repulsive vulgarian. Please try to keep your obscene thoughts to your-self, or I shall call the authorities.

LIMBIC: I've had it with you two. I'm trying to take care of the kids, while one of you is out raving and the other one is always criticizing.

Even though we ended up with the squashed-up brains, Mother Nature, as usual, compensates for the screw-ups so, in spite of these three unlikely bedfellows, we've been running fairly smoothly up until now. The brain stem has obviously been doing what it's supposed to, because we're all still breathing and breeding. The limbic system is functioning just fine because we have hot and cold running emotions and keep our kids, even though they suck us dry. The neocortex is in use because we're civilized and know how to use a hankie.

You can't categorize these three brains as good or bad; they're all useful, depending on the circumstances. Even if you'd like to dump the more primitive two, you can't, because they're there for a reason. You'll need the limbic one when 'Slasher man' leaps from a hedge (though if it then warns you to avoid all hedges in future, we have a problem). The reptilian 'grunt' brain also has its moments (*see* porno).

With training, you can start to play these three brains separately as three different notes, rather than slamming down on all three in a discord. The more you practise, the easier it gets to play the separate keys.

The Sympathetic and Parasympathetic Nervous Systems

In the limbic area, there's a small, almond-shaped cluster of neurons called the amygdala. It's the emergency button for our fight, flight or freeze response, among other strong emotions. More recent research shows that emotions aren't restricted to the amygdala but are dispersed throughout other areas across the brain. However, let's keep it simple for now and say that, millions of years ago, the amygdala emergency button worked like a dream; when there was danger it would help us to 'man up' to take on our foe by triggering a series of chemical messengers to activate what is known as our endocrine system (our inbuilt chemistry). The result of what happens is not dissimilar to what Heisenberg did in *Breaking Bad* when he cooked up the blue crystal meth and then had Jesse distribute it . . . but in this case it's not meth, it's the hormones cortisol and adrenaline (these can be toxic at excessive levels). Jesse (the pituitary gland) then deals these class-A hormones to his idiot sidekick (the adrenal gland), who then sells them to the street dealers (every organ in your body), who then push them to even the tiniest little blood vessels (the street kids). What I've just described is actually the workings of your sympathetic nervous system . . . and also the plot of *Breaking Bad*.

You'd think 'sympathetic' means you're feeling really sorry for yourself; sending sympathy cards with little crying puppies on the front saying, 'I'm sooooo saweeey' to all of your organs. Strangely, this isn't the case; the sympathetic nervous system, prompted by the amygdala, makes your insides scream bloody murder. Chemicals such as adrenaline increase your heartbeat and your blood pressure. Cortisol suppresses your immune system (to reduce inflammation from potential wounds) and feeds back to the amygdala that there's an emergency . . . which starts the whole cycle over again and produces more of these toxic hormones . . . and so it continues. This is why we get stressed about stress, or anxious about being anxious, and of course feelings introduce thoughts and so rumination begins.

When we're in the sympathetic nervous system the body starts to shut down in order to save energy and use what's left to get the hell out of there, stick around and kick ass . . . or, if you're a loser, freeze like a rabbit in the headlights just before you turn into roadkill. In those states, your reproductive and digestive systems also close up shop, because sex and snacking are really not necessary in an emergency situation. No one wants to be killed with their pants down, or mid-sandwich.

None of these processes takes place in order to spite you; they're to give you some mojo, to keep you alive at all costs. However, emotionally, you're getting even more frightened, because everything in you is in full 'call to arms' mode, so the stress keeps pumping, the brain is flooded with cortisol and you're now like a terrified elephant, rampaging and out of control.

If the sympathetic state persists, the neurons wither and die, especially those in the areas responsible for memory. This is why, when you're stressed, you can't remember anything. Your mind goes blank and, on a bad day, you can't even remember why you're stressed.

Cortisol weakens the neurons' ability to connect to each other in the hippocampus, preventing them from growing. With all this neuronal death, it's no wonder you become trapped in habitual negative thinking, which snowballs into rumination: 'Everyone hates me. I'm a flop. Why, why, why did I get stuck with being me? Why can't I be someone else? I can't be someone else because I'm a flop. Who would want me to be like them? Then they'd be a flop, too . . .' This litany of misery can go on for days.

Every thought produces biochemical reactions in the brain, which match a feeling in the body. When you think happy thoughts, the body feels good, thanks to the power of dopamine; you think sad, you feel sad. The brain picks up bodily emotions and translates them into thoughts. It's like a cat chasing its tail: feelings to thinking, thinking to feelings,

feelings to . . . it's endless. (In Chapter 5 I'll discuss how, when you send your focus into the body and keep it there by means of training your attention, you can stop this loop tape. Once your attention is focused on a bodily feeling, the thoughts lose their power.)

The only way to break out of this frenzy of self-loathing is somehow to lower the stress levels so the body can get back to its baseline state, with everything in balance.

When you manage to reduce the level of stress, you shift into your opposite system, the parasympathetic nervous system, which lowers your temperature, your heartbeat and your blood pressure and re-routes energy back into the brain and organs. It signals to your body that there's nothing to be afraid of: have sex, eat food and come into your right mind. All is forgiven.

The bonus of learning to self-regulate is that you develop the skill to choose which nervous system you want to be in. If you need your high-octane state to give a traffic warden some attitude when they stick a parking ticket on your windshield and you were only one minute late, then go ahead and let that sympathetic nervous system rip. But when the situation is resolved and you want to stop yourself from rehashing the ticket story all day, dumping your anger on your friends and stoking your fury even more, then you can switch to your parasympathetic nervous system.

The problem is that our default state (even when we're just shooting the breeze or mind-wandering) is the sympathetic nervous system. Our inherent disposition is to think negatively, because unconsciously we're always on the lookout for trouble, continuously churning over problems, worrying, brooding . . . Once in a while a wonderful memory will pop up, but then usually we'll be sad again because it's over. You're in palpitations of excitement about your upcoming wedding, and a few seconds later you're worrying whether you've got the right fish forks or . . . man. This ruminative daydreaming is activated in the self-referential network, where it's all about 'me'. There are various regions in this network that are responsible for the many 'me's: a narrative self, a conceptual self, a bodily self, a language area (the source of self-talk.) So this is the human condition when left to its own devices: it's all about me, me, me.

One of the physical areas of the brain that inhibits self-involvement is known as the dorsolateral prefrontal cortex (DLPFC): the mummy or daddy of the mind, which takes charge when you get too silly or too crazy. It is also involved in the act of deciding, when you have a moral dilemma, which way to go. It's part of your brain which I

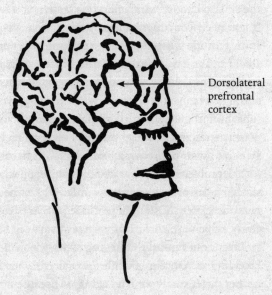

Dorsolateral
prefrontal
cortex

My illustration.

imagine as two reins holding back a wild horse that is always on the verge of bolting. Mindfulness strengthens the DLPFC so it becomes easier to pull back your focus, to keep it on the task at hand and not be torn away by irrelevant thoughts.

We need a sense of self for three things: self-reflection, consistency and identity. (It would be terrible if you thought you were Napoleon, as some do; but they're locked away.) But this sense of self backfires when we start to compare ourselves to other people, as it then creates a sense of inferiority and shame, and low self-esteem.

Using fMRI (functional magnetic resonance imaging, which shows an image of the living brain and records which regions are active during a mental activity), you can see this happening whenever you intentionally move from scattergun thinking back to the task at hand. Think of this as an ability to move focus from the dictatorial mind to a more democratic way of thinking where you have a choice of which information you want to pay attention to and which to ignore.

If you don't like the reining-in image, here's another one I use. I picture someone putting their hands on my head in the region of the DLPFC and cradling it until the turmoil inside settles down. (You don't need to be Freud to guess that those hands just might symbolize the gentle mommy I never had.) When certain areas of the brain are soothed and the self-talk quietens down it's because this DLPFC is becoming denser with neural connections and therefore strengthened. There's recent evidence that, even after only an eight-week course of mindfulness, a substantial increase in these neural connections can be observed in an MRI scanner.

This doesn't mean that by using those reins or hands you have suppressed the self-talk (you need it to exist), but it means that it's less intrusive and that you're in control of its volume. The thoughts are no longer the stars of the show;

they're just actors who can be told when to exit or enter by you, the director.

More on the Brain Terrain

Why am I using all this neuroscientific lingo? Well, I'm a pragmatist. If my boiler is broken, I want to know why. I don't bring in a healer or a reiki master; I want a plumber in there to tell me what valves do what and why. Same with all these brain regions, zones and circuits: just to know they have a name is reassuring and warms my aorta. (And I get off on the fancy names . . . forgive me.)

The following are some of the areas in the brain that are affected by the practice of mindfulness.

Grey Matter A substance known as 'gloop' holds most of the actual brain cells, and if it increases in density, it means that there's an increase in connectivity between the neurons. Think of it as a muscle. The more you use a specific region, the thicker the grey matter becomes. If there's more grey matter, it means more neurons, and their density determines the vitality and strength of your thinking.

Mindfulness promotes the growth of grey matter in many regions of the brain. Here are a few of them:

Prefrontal Cortex (PFC) The more you practise mindfulness, the more grey stuff grows here – so now you're in your right mind.

Amygdala As the size of the PFC increases, the amygdala shrinks with mindfulness practice. Not only does it shrink; in addition, the functional connections between the amygdala and the PFC are weakened. This allows for less reactivity and more adeptness at paying attention and in concentration.

Insula This area gives you a visceral awareness of your senses, in contrast to you thinking about them. The more you practise mindfulness, the bigger the anterior insula grows, and the reason we want a big, healthy one is because it creates metacognition (the ability to stand back and watch your thoughts and feelings). Each time you focus on a sense (touch, hearing, taste, smell, sight), the insula is activated. The stronger the insula becomes, the easier it is to anchor the mind and quieten it down.

Hippocampus MRI shows that, with mindfulness, there's an increased concentration of grey matter, as well as structural changes in the hippocampus. The birth of these new neurons improves mental dexterity, flexibility of thinking and memory recall.

Anterior Cingulate Cortex (ACC) A star in the show as far as self-regulation and paying attention is concerned. It detects when your focus has drifted away from where you want it to be. Whenever you notice that this has happened, this area grows stronger, making it easier for you to switch focus from the thinking mind to the feeling mind. It is the master of being able to hold focus and not be torn away by distractions. It encircles the amygdala, so it can control our distress and divert attention to somewhere else that's safer. The strengthening of the ACC with regard to attention regulation by the practice of mindfulness could prove promising for those who suffer from Attention Deficit Hyperactivity Disorder (ADHD), and, possibly, bipolar disorder, though there isn't any specific evidence yet. However, there is evidence of improvement in attention.

Temporo-parietal Junction As mentioned earlier, mindfulness produces a greater sense of bodily awareness when you move your focus into the body. This can be witnessed in brain imaging by the fact that, during mindfulness practice, grey matter can be seen to have increased in an area known as the temporo-parietal junction, which is where you get your sense of bodily self. This is key to helping individuals with borderline personality disorders and is also relevant to people with eating disorders and those suffering addiction.

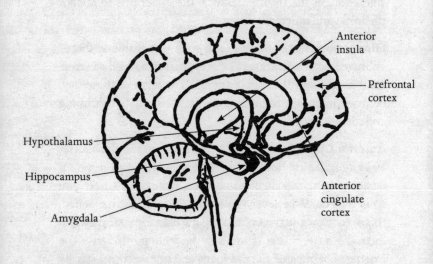

My illustration of the regions mentioned above – it's a brain cut in half (don't try it on yourself).

Parasympathetic Nervous System Mindfulness is associated with increased parasympathetic activity and decreased sympathetic activity, which leads to a lower heart rate, lower blood pressure and breathing rate and less muscle tension.

So, really, what I've been yapping on about is that by

learning to emotionally regulate ourselves through mindfulness practice, we're re-routing our more primitive reactions to the higher brain. We can see evidence that the activity of the prefrontal cortex increases and, at the same time, the activity in the amygdala decreases. The opposite of this (less prefrontal and more amygdala activity) results in an increase in the severity of social phobias, and to anxiety.

For evidence of all of the above, among many other research articles you can read, these conclusions can be found in 'How Does Mindfulness Meditation Work from a Conceptual and Neural Perspective?', (Britta K. Hölzel et el., in *Perspectives on Psychological Sciences* 2011 6: 537, at: http://pps.sagepub.com/content/6/6/537).

For those of you who, like me, love a bit of evidence, here comes some more.

The first researcher to report the effect of meditation on brain structure was Harvard neuroscientist Sara Lazar, a researcher in the psychiatry department at Massachusetts General Hospital. Using fMRI, she found that the amount of grey matter in the insula increased in those who practised mindfulness.

Lazar also did an experiment in which she obtained highly detailed pictures of the brains of twenty meditators and compared them with images obtained from a control group of twenty non-meditators. The meditators had practised for an average of about nine years, and spent, on average, a little less than an hour a day meditating. All were Westerners living in the United States and working in typical jobs. The non-meditators were local volunteers, matched to the meditators for characteristics like age and gender but with no experience in yoga or meditation.

When the brain images of the two groups were compared, Lazar found that particular areas in the brains of the meditators were significantly thicker than the same areas in non-meditators.

Lazar and her associates also recently reported that the region of the brain most associated with emotional reactivity and fear – the amygdala – has decreased grey-matter density in meditators, who experience less stress. Laboratory testing can measure the ways in which the mind becomes stronger with practice, and the mind demonstrates significant improvements over a relatively brief period of time.

You might have noticed that these findings refer to meditation rather than mindfulness. Though they could be considered similar, meditation is more of an exercise whereas mindfulness is using that exercise to build up the skill of being able to pay attention in the moment, without judgement, in daily life.

And here's the bit that whets my whistle: Cliff Saron of the University of California looked at the effect of meditation on a molecule involved with the longevity of cells:

The molecule in question was an enzyme called telomerase, which lengthens DNA segments at the ends of chromosomes. The segments ensure the stability of genetic material during cell division. They shorten every time a cell divides, and when their length decreases below a critical threshold the cell stops dividing and gradually enters a state of senescence. Compared with a control group, the meditators who showed the most pronounced reductions in physiological stress also had higher telomerase activity. These findings suggest that mindfulness training might slow processes of cellular ageing among some practitioners.

For me, if I only have a little spare time in my day, the choice between tightening my bum or doing some MBCT to lengthen and improve my life is a no-brainer. (Don't despair: in my six-week course in Chapter 5, I'll show you how to get the tight bum at the same time as practising mindfulness. It's win-win.)

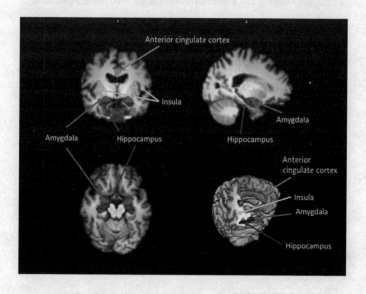

I thought I'd get my own brain scanned to show that we're all the same under our various façades. My areas just happen to be more attractive than most other people's. Here's my brain . . .

Why We Need to Do Something Quick:
Diseases Both Physical and Mental

- 90 per cent of people seeking medical care are doing so because of stress-related disorders linked to extreme emotions, rather than actual illnesses
- 40 million workers in the European Union are affected by work-related stress
- The cost of working days lost in Europe as a result of stress is estimated to be more than 20 billion euros

Although short-term stress can benefit the immune system and speed up its responses (for example, healing wounds), chronic stress worsens the impact of infectious diseases and gives you a predisposition to many chronic diseases and other conditions.

- Decreased libido
- Dementia
- Diabetes
- Digestive disorders
- Hardening of the arteries
- Heart disease
- Infertility
- Memory loss
- Mental disorders
- Obesity
- Premature ageing
- Specific cancers
- Viral infections

Compared to the damage caused by stress, smoking might actually be less harmful . . . don't say I said that, but I did.

The breakdown of the immune system is the culprit behind many of the diseases above, and stress contributes to this by disrupting the interaction between the nervous and the immune systems. The purpose of mindfulness is to lower stress levels by altering our relationship to stress for the better. A large body of research documents the effectiveness of MBCT in the treatment of substance abuse, for eating disorders and chronic pain, to improve immune function and reduce blood pressure and cortisol levels. Not only is MBCT successful in the treatment of disorders, it has positive effects on psychological well-being.

Let me run through some of the consequences of stress in more detail.

Addiction

Let's make one thing clear: we're not just addicted to drugs, sex or alcohol, we can also get addicted to our thoughts and feelings of panic, anxiety and despair. Just to get another hit, we might hunt for people who create those feelings we're addicted to; we always find the perfect perpetrator. Some people can't tell if they have a relationship with someone because they like them or just because this person keeps the chemicals they're addicted to bubbling in their veins. Even humiliation can be addictive.

Whether it's a recreational drug or an emotional drug, you become addicted when certain chemicals cross the synapses between neurons via certain receptors. These receptors wait for the right chemical to come along then work like keyholes, waiting for the right keys (the chemicals) to click into them. It's not a one size fits all; only certain chemicals can go through certain receptors, or keyholes. Serotonin can only be taken in by a serotonin receptor. They're very monogamous, those receptors.

If you start to generate excessive amounts of dopamine, which makes you feel invincible and powerful, you'll want more. Eventually, those receptors become desensitized through overuse and you won't get the wallop you used to get. Enter cocaine, which, coincidentally, has a similar key to dopamine, to fit into the perfectly matched dopamine receptor keyhole. If you can't get your own stash of dopamine, you'll turn to the next-best thing: recreational drugs. And of course you'll always need more, as those receptors lose their mojo . . . such is the bitch of addiction: it doesn't end until you end it or it ends you.

I, personally, had a penchant for rage. (I still do, but I'm more aware that, when I let it out to play, I get a toxic backlash and this is why, to this day, I have acid reflux.) So I just dream about it now, the old quickening of the heart, the feel of my body turning into The Alien, my teeth bared and snarling. I used to create situations to get yet another hit of that rage, and all of this is still embedded in my brain. I still get up almost every morning and scan for whoever I'm furious at. Who can I call and abuse? Even if it's a poor, innocent employee of a company that sent me the wrong-sized duvet. (I wanted a queen-size, not a single, for God's sake.)

I especially love those calls because I can feel the salesperson quivering and trying to stay nice, which enrages me even more. Anger is my fingerprint, but the less I act on it, the less addictively feverish it becomes, like a memory that's fading. This doesn't mean I've turned beige, I still have the residue of fury up my sleeve, but now I use it only on occasions when my anger is appropriate, as in when someone's taking my parking space on purpose.

Just as I've tried to stop my traffic-warden-attacking habit, you can change the long-term effect of your body's response to stress by learning to regulate your basic fight, flight and freeze reactions. Stress isn't always a response to an emergency or a disaster; it builds up from small day-to-day tensions there might be at your workplace, in your home life or your community, and can have long-term physical and mental consequences. Stress levels can also be made worse by a rich diet, by smoking, drinking alcohol . . . anything that whacks up your cortisol. The way in which a person interprets an event, along with their general state of physical health, is not determined completely by genetic factors but by behavioural and lifestyle choices. In other words, don't blame your mother for giving you the genes that led to your crack habit.

Type 2 Diabetes

For emergencies (fight or flight), we need to increase the level of glucose in our bloodstream to give us energy, but if the stress lasts too long the body can no longer take in the glucose and the result is diabetes. (Insulin regulates glucose and, when it depletes, the cells starve.)

So the thing that helps us in the short term becomes damaging over time. One bit of chocolate is good, but a chocolate fountain with a straw next to your bed isn't.

Obesity

During a period of stress, as I mentioned above, the digestive system shuts down, because you need all your energy for flight or fight and there's no time to think about lunch. When sugar levels rise over time, insulin, as with diabetes, becomes resistant to glucose and glucose can't be absorbed. This means that you eventually end up on one of those TV shows where they need to take the roof off your house and have a helicopter airlift you out of your spaghetti-filled bed.

Infertility

If you're suffering too much stress, your reproductive system shuts down. During that time, for men, making testosterone and sperm aren't at the top of their list; when running for their lives, the last thing they need is an erection. And you don't need science to tell you that, when a woman is stressed, she doesn't feel like sex. This is because inconveniences such as ovulation, menstruation, growing a foetus and breast-feeding will only slow her down. (There are, however, exceptions to this rule: a woman who, when being chased by a predator, will not run . . . but slows down and takes time to wax her legs and put on tantalizing underwear; she is not going to flee or fight the predator, she is going to date him.)

Cancer

One possible connection between stress and the develop-ment of a cancer is that stress inhibits the immune system, which, ordinarily, can detect early tumours and fight them.

Heart Disease

In the short term, when we're stressed, our blood pressure and our heart rate increase and we manufacture more glu-cose to gain some energy. In the long term, the repeated surges of blood pressure and heart rate can create a predis-position to heart disease, and also strokes.

Memory Loss and Age-related Diseases

One sign of ageing is the thinning of the prefrontal cortex. This is slowed down by the growth of grey matter, which promotes longevity and creates a more agile, sharper and more energized way of thinking compared to someone with only a piddly spoonful of grey matter.

Depression and Other Mental Disorders

No one knows for sure how much psychological illness is due to nature and how much to nurture, but, in a nutshell, if you have the genes for depression and have a great life, they may never turn on. On the other hand, if your parents are wilder than hyenas or something terrible happens to you in life, *BOOM!*, you just might find yourself with a mental disorder. There are chemicals that may contribute to depression, but none of this has been proven 100 per cent. Adrenaline makes you feel energetic, but cortisol and, particularly, glucocorticoid hormones deplete energy and cause you to feel that death grip of depression. Those glucocorticoids also lower the production of dopamine, reducing your sense of motivation and pleasure.

Stress reduces serotonin (the big gun in promoting perkiness) and can cause a loss of interest in being alive.

Let's just say that stress comes with the territory of mental disarray because the endless parade of shame and self-loathing means that toxic chemicals are running riot. And what turns them on? Is it a predator with razor fangs? Is it a nuclear weapon heading for your back garden? No, it's because your thoughts are on that spin cycle of doom: rumination. This mode of thinking can lead to anxiety, panic attacks and depression.

The Stress of Stress

If you suffer from any physical disease and add stress, it can exacerbate the problem, or even create a completely new illness; you may have a heart attack because you're so worried about your shingles. This second hit of stress from ruminating about your illness or injury can cause limitless damage. Mindfulness can help you calm your thoughts down to avoid the second hit. The ladling of stress on top of shame, on top of the illness is what ultimately crushes you rather than the physical or mental problems themselves.

Saving the Day: Neuroplasticity

At this point you may be throwing your arms up, thinking, 'What am I supposed to do with this information about stress? I am the way I am. So what if I'm addicted to my habits – does that make me a bad person?' This is the equivalent of saying, 'I can't do anything, I'm a slob, it's my destiny, and it's written in the stars.' As if a slob fairy came to you in the night when you were asleep and trashed your house. There is no destiny about it. Even with no arms and no legs, you can still clean your room – my mother used to vacuum with her teeth: let's learn from her.

Nowadays, we know that your genes give you the basics (let's think of them as a pot of potential chemicals and a vague blueprint of neural connections) but that they can be altered. Even when you're in the womb, everything – and I mean everything – you experience reconfigures the neural patterns which reflect how you think, feel and behave. The brain is never static; the patterns and connections are in constant flux, in more possible configurations than there are stars in the universe. There is no finished model called 'you'; we're all in a state of flux. This is the constant shape-shifting known as neuroplasticity.

Neuroplasticity is the capacity to create new neural connections. Our brains are like sponges that change shape with every thought and experience. Even after reading this sentence, your brain wiring will have changed.

Our brains are made up of trillions of intricately connected neurons that are in continual communication, sending electrochemical signals to each other. We can't eavesdrop on what they're communicating about, but if you place someone inside an fMRI scanner and ask them to do specific tasks or think specific thoughts, the neurons in various areas are activated, and this gives us some clues as to what's going on upstairs. There can be a whole 'Kanye West on tour' lightshow going on in your brain while you're just sitting around having a pedicure.

It's like Pass the Parcel. Each neuron passes on information – not some crap plastic toy wrapped in newspaper, but crucial information – via electric currents, triggering the release of specific chemicals, or neurotransmitters. They bathe the brain in various recipes, which make you do what you do, think what you think and feel what you feel. If you repeat certain behaviours, thoughts or feelings, the neural connections associated with them become harder wired, and the harder wired they are, the more you'll repeat the same behaviours, thoughts or feelings. *Et voilà*, a habit is created, which limits your view of the world and of yourself.

Now that we know the brain is in a constant state of change, it's clear that by altering our thinking we can change the landscape and break unhelpful patterns and the production of chemicals that accompany them.

Here's a theory on why focusing attention might affect neuroplasticity. A part of your brain called the nucleus basalis (it's adjacent to the brain stem) has little neural spikes that secrete a chemical throughout the cortex when it's stimulated. (I won't even tell you the name: it's way too long.) This chemical juice can strengthen the connections between neurons once they've been activated. When we focus our attention, the stuff they squirt out produces neuroplasticity. This could be one reason why the power of thinking physically changes our brain. But how can we do it? I bring the topic back to that old brain sculptor: MBCT.

How Mindfulness Enhances Neuroplasticity

When we practise mindfulness, we can take advantage of neuroplasticity to release ourselves from the bondage of our habits. To do that, we need to learn how to use our brains effectively, to strengthen certain neural connections and break others, turn the chemicals up or down to make them work for us and not against us.

Some people don't bother learning about the hardware that runs their computer or study the engine in their car. I so understand: it's boring, and who has time? The rub is: when the engine goes you can get another car, but when we break down there is no newer model to replace the old one.

Now that we know about neuroplasticity, we can no longer say that we can't change, that we are what we are and we can't help it; we're just a bigger version of the original baby. By learning about the brain and how malleable it is, we can understand that the brain changes when we change our thinking. We do this by questioning our habits of thinking and making conscious decisions about how we want to live our lives. We can intentionally redecorate our neural interiors to throw out the old patterns and update and improve on them.

Animals do the same old, same old, until evolution moves them on by giving them a hump to deal with a lack of water, or a long neck to get to the leaves at the top of the tree. Animals don't have to come up with these things; evolution does it for them. We, however, have the potential to use our thoughts consciously to evolve because we can advance and improve ourselves by our thoughts alone; we don't have to wait around until it happens to us. The brain isn't designed to stop learning, and so when we stop upgrading it the wiring gets locked and we resort to being on automatic pilot and to our old habits. To evolve, we have to break away from genetic habits and use what we've learnt as a species purely as a base to work from.

If evolution is our contribution to the future, then our free will is how we initiate the process.

This is a quote from one of the greatest experts on the neuroscience of mindfulness, Richard Davidson.

There is a promising science emerging on how mindfulness 'works' at the level of brain/ bodily physiology and functioning: its findings are starting to mirror the reports from subjective experience (i.e. what people 'feel' is happening).

Recent developments in neuroscience have demonstrated that the structure and function of the brain is by no means fixed in childhood, and that brains remain 'neuroplastic', i.e. changeable, throughout our lives. An increasing number of brain imaging/ MRI studies of the impact of mindfulness suggest that it reliably and profoundly alters the structure and function of the brain to improve the quality of both thought and feeling. Mindfulness meditation appears to reshape the neural pathways, increasing the density and complexity of connections in areas associated with both cognitive abilities such as attention, self-awareness and introspection, and emotional areas connected with kindness, compassion and rationality, while decreasing activity and growth in those areas involved in anxiety, hostility, worry and impulsivity.

Not to push the point too hard, but here are a few more reasons to think about practising mindfulness.

The US National Institute of Health published the outcome of research on meditators versus non-meditators. 'The results showed a massive reduction in mortality compared with those who didn't meditate. The meditation group showed a 23 per cent decrease in mortality over a nineteen-year period. There was also a 30 per cent decrease in rates of cardiovascular mortality.'

Other ways to live longer (if mindfulness isn't for you) is to have a lot of friends around, marry someone who makes you laugh, keep learning, exercise, eat broccoli and don't smoke.

4

A Depressing Interlude

I wrote the last few words up to about here in my book on 9 November 2014. I picked it up again on 25 January 2015. In that gap of time, after a respite of seven years, I had another episode of depression. I was never cocky enough to imagine that it would never return; I knew it would. I just thought that, with the mindfulness, I'd be able to feel it coming. That's one of the many bitches of depression: because it's your brain that is ill, you can't stand back and take an objective, clear view like you could if your foot was hanging off at the ankle. I knew there was no magic pill; all I wanted was to be ready for it when it pounced out of the shadows again. But of course it moves into you so slowly and stealthily that you think it's just who you've become; like a wrinkle you get used to and now think was always there.

I was in America to promote my book and perform my show. Working there has never been good for my health. There are triggers everywhere; mental booby-traps. I associate being in America with it being the land of my failure. Due to early parental mismanagement, I only ever did one thing successfully, and that was to get out. I'm not saying my parents shouldn't have emigrated to America, because if they hadn't I wouldn't be here, tapping on these keys, but whenever I hit those sunny shores, I'm overwhelmed with

the feeling that I'm a big disappointment to everyone, starting with the guys at customs control. I won't go into what
happened during the book tour – I'll have flashbacks and be
re-traumatized . . . oh, okay, I'll tell you.

I started my journey to publicise my book *Sane New World* in
New York on 5 November 2014. Everyone tells me they love
New York; to me, it's a gang rape on the senses. I want to
confess to war crimes after being kept up all night, listening
to trash trucks clanging and endless honking. I took the sub-
way late one night after a show, waited two hours for the
right train and witnessed bedlam; feral people howled like
wolves and some guy, completely naked, was playing air
banjo. When the train finally came at 1.30 a.m., I stood
crammed into it like the way they cram battery chickens
into boxes when they're being shipped off to be executed. I
went to Broadway, where tourists from hell elbow you off
the sidewalk to get in front. (In front of what, I don't know.)
Imagine every race in the world elbowing each other. It's
like the Olympics, where every nation brings out their best
and sharpest elbowers. It's not pretty: some countries end up
lying in the gutter; others are crushed by the stronger ones. I
kept hearing the English saying, 'Sorry, sorry'; they were
almost going backwards they were so bad at pushing. To calm
myself down, I went to a nail bar. All of America has been hit
by a plague of nail bars where they try to tear your cuticles off
and sandpaper the bottom of your feet. (This is a common
method of torture used in Guantanamo Bay.) I asked for a
back massage and was skinned by a man in two minutes.

From New York, I flew to Los Angeles, where Carrie
Fisher interviewed me about my book and, because I've
known her for thirty-five years and love her, it was like having sex in public. That was the last of the good experiences.

A Depressing Interlude

The following morning I was picked up for my first interview in LA. The drive took one hour to get to a mall filled with yet more nail bars. There, among them, was a shoddy vitamin shop. I walked through it, and in the back behind a beaded curtain was my interviewer: a withered man with three hairs and dandruff holding a microphone. He opened with his theory that you can cure prostate cancer with green tea. He then shouted, 'Make-up!' as if it was a standing joke, because of course there weren't even any chairs, let alone a make-up room. The man who held the home camera to film us was near death, his hands shaking so badly I'm sure we looked like a blur. The first question was: which supplements or tinctures did I think cured mental illness? I mentioned something about the brain, and he had no idea what I was referring to. There was a lunatic called Mr Chuckles, wearing a hat with a propeller on top, waiting to go on after me. He told me he was a comedy writer, like me. He had a Looney Tunes smile and a voice like he was sucking on helium. On the way out I was given some free cancer-cure vitamins and a book called *I Eat Green Food*. The person who was supposed to drive me back ran out of electricity for her electric car and needed to find a plug. That was it. I begged Mr Chuckles to give me a ride back to LA.

My next interview was with a corpse: a woman who had died ten years ago was glued upright in her chair. Her first words were something about lamb chops. I have no idea what else was said. Afterwards, I was driven to the wrong terminal so I missed a plane and had to get a later one that landed in Philadelphia at one in the morning. When I got to the airport hotel they told me they were overbooked, so they got someone to drive me to another hotel on another galaxy in the middle of nowhere. It was worth it to hear one of the great lines of my life, from my driver: 'Well, the good news is it's near a Denny's.' (Denny's, for those who aren't in the know, is a place to get eggs all night after you've been up snorting horse tranquillizers.) My room had footprints on the walls and on the ceiling and deep, dark stains on everything.

Having finished a triumphant book tour (I sold four books), I went to Harvard, where I was to do my *Sane New World* show. Luckily, the theatre I was performing in was about six feet from the apartment I was given, so even I could manage to navigate that gap to get backstage. I know it didn't help that the audiences were thinning each night. I coined a new phrase for it: 'the balding venue'. I'd see the little bemused, but not so amused, faces of the members of the audience the moment the show began. They didn't know when to laugh or cry, because many of my people in America (I know this from my childhood) don't know that you can do both at the same time. I knew how, because that's how I lived: by crying and laughing at the same time. It's a skill set I've always had and, fortunately, when I got to the UK I realized it had a name: irony. In retrospect, I should have held up signs during my performance reading: 'This is funny' and 'This isn't funny.' Perhaps I should have used a laugh track. One thing was certain: the show wasn't going well either. At the end of my set I'd hear a few claps and try not to burst with heartbreak. Then I'd run home and hide under the duvet.

I assumed I had that feeling of being empty and invisible because I was alone and it was snowing a lot. (See how you delude yourself when you're mentally unwell?) Each day it got worse, but I wasn't aware of what was happening, I just kept thinking it was because it was snowing harder. My fear levels went way up (why I would connect this to snow I have no idea), so much so that I shook when I had to go down the block to buy milk.

I didn't even realize I had depression when it stopped snowing. To use up the daylight hours, I'd take a taxi (I was too scared to walk) to some herbal treatment rooms I had found which had grungy, bubbling, wooden hot tubs and slime on the floor. Everyone was really nice and didn't question why I spent my days sitting in reception. There was a woman at the desk who, normally, I'd have used as material for an episode of *Absolutely Fabulous*; she looked like she was wearing a dream-catcher and had a voice that sounded like windchimes. In my current state I loved her because she was nice to me, asking me every few minutes if I wanted any Yrikikimototo bark tea from Papua New Guinea. She never asked me why I sat in reception for seven days, with no appointment. That's how spiritual – and bad at her job – she was.

Did I mention that my computer broke down? I went to the Genius bar and they said it was a mystery. Like a computer poltergeist had got into my hard drive and wiped everything I'd ever written. Maybe I unconsciously decided to keep it company, so my brain also got wiped. I bought a new computer in a mall and then decided to buy food from those stores that have bowling alleys full of salad bars. I ended up walking through the streets of Cambridge, Massachusetts with my two bags; one holding the computer and all the accessories, the other 500lbs of frozen yogurt and Oreos. At last a taxi picked me up, and I spent the rest of the evening knocking on doors, asking if I lived there.

Eventually, it ended. I don't know how I got back to the UK, but a week later I found myself on a flight to Norway. I had accepted this gig six months earlier, when it was warm and sunny.

Now it's early December and I'm on a plane, mentally gone but holding on to a ticket and a change of underwear. After many hours and a few internal transfers, I realize we're going way into the Arctic Circle to a place I didn't even know you could travel to without a husky. When I get off the plane it is pitch black (it always is, I found out later). Then, when I leave the airport, my luggage is torn out of my hands by the wind-chill factor (78,965,463) and the skin on my face is ripped off. It's like having dermabrasion with a chainsaw.

The town they take me to is not made up of cute, white clapboard houses but is a hard-core industrial oil/ fish refinery-looking thing that reminds me of Chernobyl. I'm placed in a minimalist hotel, and when I say that, I mean no furniture and long rooms like in *The Shining*. They'd given me an all-white suite with a white runway which ended in a dead plant. Did I mention that the heating didn't work and the restaurant had closed, never to be opened again?

In the morning there was no breakfast so I went into the kitchen and stole food like a squirrel. The sun never rose, not at ten in the morning or one in the afternoon: never. The wind howled all night and the rain pelted on my windows. It was like standing under Niagara Falls with a piece of aluminium foil over your head. At that point, even with the depression, I started to laugh. It felt like a tiny space or chink in my brain had opened up and let in some light. I could see what was funny about all this. I was taken to a concrete Soviet Bloc building to do my show. There I was in this depressing atmosphere, talking to about six hundred people (who were probably depressed) about depression.

When I got back to London they lost my luggage again. For no apparent reason, it had been sent to Copenhagen.

I'm sitting here now in my bedroom, feeling the darkness descend, blocking out all thought. At least when I practise mindfulness I'm able to separate myself a little from all those abusive thoughts which are trying to bomb me to total destruction. With the mindfulness practice, I can say, 'There is depression' rather than 'I'm depressed.' It's the little things that count. I'm trying to ride the wave rather than go under. Wish me luck.

Some Time Later

I don't remember much from then on, except someone suggesting I go to the Priory. I presumed I'd get a special discount for doing so much publicity for them and mentioning them in my last book. (No matter how mentally ill I am, I can always think about discounts.)

Here's where the mindfulness came in handy. This time, I knew I was ill. I knew I wasn't being a wanker and making it up. It took me a while, but I knew not to punish myself. It had only taken a few weeks to recognize my depression, rather than months, so I had done well. I submitted to the full weight of mental deadness; I gave in and just let it take me over. I succumbed, forgave myself and didn't scream at myself to 'fucking perk up'. I just accepted it. The fact that I could forgive myself for having a disease without also having to deal with the commentary savaging me for having the nerve to have something wrong with me when I have enough food to eat and an actual Prada bag was a start. In the centre of my dead brain I knew this was real and it had got me. For now.

It passed much more quickly than any of my other depressions because I knew not to get anxious about being anxious, fearful about feeling fear, or depressed about being depressed. Just by doing that I could dodge the second layer of pain, because I knew that, while the disease itself is real, that second layer is self-induced. This time, I was only in for a week, then I went home to bed and waited it out. After that, my daughter took care of me, understanding that it was too terrifying for me even to get tea. I also found out, for the first time, that I could write while being like this. So while I waited it out, not knowing if I would ever be 'me' again, I wrote this.

10 December 2014

Depressed . . . no end in sight. I suppose this is my brain saying, 'You went too far, you pushed me too far, and now I'm shutting for the season. I'm going to shut you down, make sure you can't do anything even if you try.' In a way, it's survival: when your thoughts have declared war on you and you feel friendless, hated and forgotten, the brain just shuts down, leaving a hazy blur, a fog. I've been in the fog for about a week. It feels like I've been reunited with an evil, lost relative, someone from my past I can vaguely recognize – and then it comes to me: oh yes, it's depression. I remember now. When you're well, you can't remember you ever had it. Probably your mind ingeniously erases it from your memory because it's too frightening for you to contemplate it ever coming back. And now that my depression is back in town I have that 'aha' moment that this is what it is. This feeling of being estranged from my body and mind is depression. Of course.

This time, it's different from any of my past episodes. At

this point, when I'd had depression in the past, I'd be panicking that my old self was gone – my old personality was lost and this new, deader one had come to replace it. But even in this chaos now I sort of know this is temporary, I just happen to have this disease and this loss of identity is part of it; my mind is just out of the office for a minute.

I always knew some day it would come back. I know there's no miracle cure, so I tried to get ready for it by practising mindfulness, and maybe this is why I have an overview rather than being stuck in blackness with no view.

Oh my God, does my heart go out to people with depression who have to go to work and feel what I'm feeling! To have to drag the heavy weight and then try to hide it in case people think you're wallowing in some phantom sickness. The horror that, if someone asked you to tell them what the matter was, you couldn't. No one is as cruel to those of us who have depression as ourselves. We keep ourselves going even when we're broken. It's like beating a dying animal to keep it moving. I'm amazed that so many people keep on going into work and trying to act as if everything's okay. They should be knighted or given something like a Purple Heart for their bravery, because that is the most difficult thing on earth when you're depressed: to have to keep acting like a human when you don't feel like one any more.

I'm fortunate that I can just sit this out, because I don't have a nine-to-five job. I can just lie here. I'm babysitting myself: waiting, waiting, for the gigantic thing that has blocked out the sun to move away.

I can't read, I'm not funny, I can't really speak, get up or go for a walk. But this time I'm not fearful about having depression; having studied it, I know this is what it is. Nor am I ashamed, feeling that I'm making this up and could 'snap out' of it. Fear is a symptom of the disease; I feel I'm in full emergency mode because chemicals have started to flood my brain and cause havoc. You can't think your way out of this disease: it has you; you don't have it. I have to keep telling myself that this is not my fault, that there is no difference between the mental and physical, it's a reality that our brain and body are symbiotically interconnected. This is why there's such a stigma about mental illness: it's not taken seriously. But imagine if I reacted to someone telling me they had Lupus (the disease everyone has, every week, on *House*) by saying, 'Oh, well, that's only physical – snap out of it.'

I did force myself to go for a walk yesterday, and it felt as if, with every step, I would fall through the earth. I tried to be like a good mother; I kept saying to myself how well I was doing, that even to be outside was a triumph. So I'm still scared, but not scared that I'm losing my mind, because I know this is depression and these are the traits that come with it. I know this monster, I've studied it and I know how deep its roots are in me, leaching my energy out of me. I know all this, and yet the anthem of all depressives plays in my mind, repeating, 'How long will this last? How long will this last?' It's hard for me to write this and come up with words and sentences, because it feels like there's no one at the wheel of the ship. I'm pushing myself to keep going so I can remember what it feels like, and so that everyone else who suffers with this knows to be able to say, 'This is not my imagination. I am not being self-indulgent.'

19 December 2014

A week ago, I left the institution for the bemused and bewildered. The dictator who lives in my head still barks and bullies me to get off my ass, but this time I have an excuse, a note from my shrink that verifies I'm sick. I don't have to go to school, or anywhere else. I'm still swamped by those recordings in my brain: every time I get a blast of one of those 'I should's or a memory of screwing up it feels like someone's sticking a syringe in my heart and squirting something toxic straight into an artery. I try to deflect or accept those painful 'I should's. It's if I'm babysitting myself, trying to soothe a sick child.

21 December 2014

When you have a physical illness, there's often an explanation. You might say to yourself, 'Of course I feel terrible, I have an infection/ a virus' (pick one). One thing you could say about dementia is that at least you might be the last to know that something's wrong; with depression, you're completely aware that you're gone and that's what's left of you: a zombie who can only steer you into the bathroom and find food. That's about it.

25 January 2015

I woke up, and it was gone!! As sneakily as the monster came in, it left and I could almost imagine it was a bad dream – but then I realized I had really *not* been outside and had physical evidence to prove it: bedhead hair and rotting pyjamas. Like an animal after a long hibernation, I peeked out and saw the scenery clearly, and there was light. Then the phone rang, and it was the publisher of this book, who said, 'Are you finished with depression?' And before I could answer, she said, 'Good, your new deadline is the first of July.'

5

The Six-week Mindfulness Course

Points to Remember

With mindfulness, unlike anything else you do in your life, there is no getting it right. Drop the idea of pleasing Teacher or Mummy or the boss: they can't harm you – the tests are over now and, this time, you can't fail. Even when you're doing it wrong, it's always right because you're not trying to make anything better or to empty your mind of thoughts, it's just about noticing what's going on in your mind. This six-week mindfulness course is aimed at people who want to be able to fall asleep at night and to be able to focus on the task at hand when they're awake. These exercises don't have to be done in an isolated place, in a darkened room with a single piece of gluten-free incense, or on a meditation cushion. I encourage you to incorporate these exercises into your real life, because that's where you'll be using them.

And one last point: You don't have to live in a continual state of mindfulness; it would take ten years to leave your house, let alone put on your socks. These are just exercises, and you practise them for a limited period of time. Eventually, with your new muscles, mindfulness spills into your life and you'll become the conductor of the orchestra, not just some piddly triangle-player stuffed at the back. I'll go into this later in the course, but you can also practise anywhere and at any time.

WEEK ONE:
Noticing and Waking Up

I've talked about paying attention; now, I'm going to tell you how to do it. This first week, I'll be weaning you off autopilot by making you aware of how much time you spend on it. I will bring you to your senses.

This first session starts with understanding what I'm talking about when I say that mindfulness is all about noticing and accepting whatever's happening, in the moment. I hear you say, 'I'm always noticing – what an obvious thing to say.' As I explained in Chapter 2, autopilot is a useful tool for making life easier to get through, but in using it you may miss the ride. So this week's exercise is about just noticing when you're on autopilot, not beating yourself up about it.

I know the thought of these exercises might make you roll your eyes, but if you don't practise them, you won't have the mental muscle to pull the joystick when the plane's going down.

After each exercise, I'll suggest some questions you may want to ponder on. My first suggestion is for you to go out and buy a diary. You can write down your reflections, just doodle on it, or if you're like me, do a 'to do' list that doesn't end . . . ever. You paid for it; you do whatever you want with it.

You should write at least a few lines in your diary each day throughout the course. I'll suggest some questions you may want to ponder on.

Exercise: Taste

Find something you enjoy putting in your mouth (within the realms of normality). Cut whatever it is (chocolate, a banana, a meatball . . . please don't make me go on, I'm sure you can come up with something yourself) into bite-sized pieces.

Place a morsel in the palm of your hand. Without feeling ridiculous (make sure no one is looking), focus on what it looks like as if you've never seen anything like it, as if you're a newborn or an alien (whichever is easier to identify with). With a sense of curiosity, *notice* the colour, the edges, the shape, the contours . . .

Slowly, slowly, track the internal sensation of lifting your arm to pick up the object and your hand to place it on your tongue. *Notice* the taste, shape, weight. (Do not swallow.)

After a minute or so, chew slowly and *notice* what sweetness or bitterness tastes like. *Notice* what the urge to swallow feels like. Finally, chew and swallow with second-by-second awareness, experience it sliding down your throat and into your stomach.

It's not about what a great swallower you are but about experiencing something you do every day by paying close attention. If at any point during the exercise your thoughts take you somewhere else, bring your focus back to the taste.

Here are questions to have in your mind.

- How was this experience different from when you eat normally?
- What did you notice about the sensations in your mouth: taste, texture, chewing, swallowing?
- Where did your mind go when you lost your focus on the taste?

Homework

Choose an activity you do regularly each day and, for a few moments while you're doing it, try to pay attention to every sensation – sight, hearing, taste, smell, touch – not thinking about it, just trying to sense it. Among other things, you might *notice* how irritating it is that I always use italics when I type *notice*. (I'll stop it now.)

You'll do the same exercise using the same activity each day of the week. Here are a few suggestions.

Showering What does the water feel like? How does 'wet' feel? Experience the movements you make while soaping up and washing the soap off again as if you've never done them before in your life. Notice when your mind takes over, then bring your focus back to the feel of showering.

Making tea Slowly, try to experience the detailed sensations of pouring, stirring, smelling, tasting and, hopefully, not burning your lips off. But if you do . . . try to sense that, too.

On your computer Tune into what the sensations are of tapping your fingers on the keys. Come off autopilot and notice when your mind begs you to type something and, when you do, come back to the feeling in your fingertips. Notice: are your shoulders humped over? (I do most of my emails in the posture of the Hunchback of Notre Dame.)

Here's a really easy one: Each day when you go through a particular doorway or sit in a certain chair, use it as a reminder to notice what's going on around you; the sounds, smells, sights and the feeling in your body. Oh, come on, you can't get away with saying you're too busy to walk through a doorway.

WEEK TWO:
Noticing Your Mind Has a Mind of Its Own

The exercises and homework from Week One are to help you begin to notice the difference between the thinking, 'doing' mind and the sensing, 'being' mind. In Week Two you will learn how to switch focus between the two. Remember: when you notice your mind has wandered, shift your focus back *without thinking you've done something wrong*. For me, this is one of the most difficult things to do, notice that my mind's snared me again; no one is as cruel a disciplinarian as me on me.

This week, you're starting your mental-fitness regime and beginning your first round of sit-ups. You're taking charge of your mind by telling it where to focus, just like a pole-vaulter knows, through practice, just where to land the pole. (Just go with the image: even I don't understand it completely.)

There are two mindfulness exercises that can be done in a variety of places: on a train (if you shut your eyes, wear earphones to make it look like you're listening to music); on a bus (same as above); having your hair cut or coloured; while you're on call waiting and they play that relentless muzak; waiting at the dentist's; at a launderette; during a boring meeting (keep your eyes open!).

Exercise: Scanning the Body

Practise for at least ten minutes (but if you have more time, go for twenty). Before you start, commit to a set time, and stick to it.

This is the essence of mindfulness. Using specific parts of

your body as an anchor, take your focus to each one so that, when your thoughts snare you (as they always will), you can take your focus back to where it was. (Count that whole process as one sit-up.) Remember: the more you repeat the action of noticing when your mind wanders and bringing it back, the stronger your 'attentional muscle' becomes.

Begin by moving your back away from the chair so that your spine is self-supporting (but not rigid), your shoulders are relaxed and your arms are resting on your lap. You can keep your eyes open or close them. If you're sitting cross-legged, sit up straight; again, shoulders relaxed.

Bring your focus to your feet, where they contact the floor – don't think about them but sense them. Keep focused and, when you notice that your mind's wandered off on some story or other, without getting irritated, bring your focus back to the soles of your feet. Remember: the point isn't to stop your mind from wandering, it's to practise being kind to yourself when you notice it's wandered.

After a few minutes, bring your attention to where your body contacts the seat of the chair, feeling the whole weight of gravity pulling you to that point. When you notice that your mind has wandered, you know what to do: don't be hard on yourself – everyone's mind does it, it's supposed to wander, so be nice and take your attention back to where you're in contact with the chair. Now let that attention go . . .

Try to remember to breathe throughout this exercise – it really helps with staying alive. And now, using your focus like a spotlight, draw it from the base of your spine, through each of your vertebrae, up to your neck. Do any areas feel held, hunched or tense? Whatever you notice, don't do anything to correct or change it; just notice it, then bring your focus back to the raw sensation.

Now send focus on the front and sides of your body, being aware of your whole torso. Let the in-breath fill it and the out-breath contract it. After a minute, let that focus go . . .

Bringing your focus to both hands – fingers, palms, the backs of the hands – notice if they're warm, cold, clawed or relaxed. Let it go . . .

Move your attention to your neck and shoulders, zooming into every area and focusing on different sensations as you scan.

Now, up to your face: your chin, lips, cheeks, nose, eyes, forehead and the top of your skull. Do you sense what facial expression you're making? When your focus drifts, as always, notice, be nice to yourself and refocus on the exact part of the face you were focusing on before.

Next, try to feel your whole body from inside: your bones and muscles, where you're in contact with the chair, the skin wrapped around you and the air outside your skin. Try to feel the breath filling your body from your toes up to the top of your head, and out again like a bellows. In the last few minutes, come back to the sense of just sitting and breathing, feet on the ground, body on the chair. Wiggle your toes, open your eyes if they were closed, get on with your day, and maybe hold on to that sense of being present.

For those of you who find it too excruciating to focus on just one part of your body at a time, just give your body a general scan, noticing if there's any tightness, discomfort, strain or numbness. It's like checking your internal weather.

Here are some sample questions for your journal.

- Which area of the body did you find the most difficult to focus on, and which was the easiest?
- Where did your mind go when it pulled you away? Were there any themes?
- What was your immediate reaction when you caught yourself mind-wandering?

Exercise: Using Sound and Breath as an Anchor

Practise this one for ten, or twenty, minutes, too.

Using your own senses for a workout is incredibly handy because, wherever you are, there they are, too. You don't need to find a gym, or a spiritual retreat in the Maldives; you're sitting on all the equipment you'll ever need.

Rather than use specific parts of your body as an anchor to stay steady, in this exercise, you're going to focus on sound and breath.

Bringing your back away from the back of your chair, your spine straight but not rigid, the crown of your head pointing to the sky, ground yourself by moving your attention to the soles of both feet, where they contact the ground. Shift your attention to the points at which your body is in contact with the chair . . . After a moment, let go of those sensations . . .

Now, move your attention to sound, so you're listening . . . to the right, to the left, in front, behind, trying to focus on the different pitches, tones and volume. After a while, you might notice that you're starting to label the sounds, or judging whether you like them or not. If you don't like them, or your mind has drifted, notice/ be nice/ refocus. This will happen hundreds of times, and hundreds of times you will gently bring your attention back to the sounds. Let the focus go . . .

Now shift your focus to your breathing. Focus on it in the same way that you let the sounds come to you. Choose an area: the nose, the back of the throat, the chest or abdomen; whichever feels the most comfortable. If it's the nose, for example, see if you can feel cool air coming in and warmer air going out. Feel the expansion and contraction in your body in as much detail as you can and let the breath breathe you rather than you controlling it. Notice what happens in the gap between the in-breath and the out-breath.

If it is too much of a challenge to keep your mind on your breath, try counting each breath up to ten and then beginning again. (In/ out is one; in/ out is two, etc.) If you get lost, just guess where you left off and start again. (Remember: this is not about getting it right but about noticing when your mind has drifted.) When you notice you're thinking in the past or the future, ruminating or mind-wandering, go back to the area you were breathing from, knowing that, wherever you are, when you notice that your mind is agitated or scattered, you can always refocus on your breathing as an anchor.

Here are a few questions for your journal.

- How was this different from the listening and breathing you do every day?
- What did you find most difficult when you were focusing on the sound? On the breath?
- When your mind snared you, do you remember where it went? Was it past or future thinking, worrying, planning, fantasizing, or was it just blank?

Homework

You can choose to do both these exercises each night over the following six days, or you can alternate them.

Now that you've learnt to focus on the breath and your body, here's a quick way to settle your mind down when the red mist of pressure frazzles your brain. It's called the three-minute breathing exercise.

Three-minute Breathing Exercise

Most people can relax watching TV, playing football or at a wine bar with friends. The problem is that, when you're about to take an exam, give a speech in front of five hundred people or have an interview for a job, you can't whip out a football or watch TV to calm yourself. However, if you have practised some mindfulness just before these nerve-racking challenges, you'll be ready to use this portable, three-minute breather. It travels wherever you go.

There are three parts to this exercise; each part lasts about a minute or so.

1. Widen your focus by tuning into every thought in your mind, inviting them all in and just letting them rip: the good, the bad, the ugly. After about a minute, let it go . . .
2. Narrow your focus to the pinpoint sensation of breathing. Zoom in on a full breath through the nose, throat, chest or abdomen, feeling your lungs expanding on the in-breath and contracting on the out-breath. After about a minute, let it go . . .
3. Widen your focus once more to your breath filling your whole body, from the top of your head, down through your body to your toes, on an inhale and on an exhale, feeling the breath empty out like a giant bellows.

Try to take a three-minute breather twice a day, particularly when you feel that your mind is sizzling from obsessive phone usage/ compulsive emailing, or from some resentment you are burning with, to give yourself a break from all the mind-chatter. I promise: after you do it, you'll feel better.

WEEK THREE:
Mindful Movement

Think of the sitting exercises above as like practising scales on a piano to tone and strengthen your ability (eventually) to play Rachmaninov with ease. A ballet dancer doesn't just do pliés at the bar in order to do better pliés but because, hopefully, one day, they're going to dance in *Swan Lake*. With the practice of mindfulness, you'll be able to apply the skills of anchoring to your daily life. (You won't, however, be asked to join the Bolshoi.)

The brain doesn't end at the neck, it continues sending messages along the spinal cord, which branches out to millions of miles of blood vessels (enough to encircle the world three times, I've been told) that carry blood to every one of your trillions of cells. There is no dividing line between where your mind ends and your body begins; your body and your mind are all of a piece, like a onesie. They are in constant communication with each other, interpreting feedback from the world outside and the world inside and creating the reality you inhabit.

Mindful movement is about how to intertwine your brain and your body – which is not, as many believe, a sack of skin that you're condemned to drag around like a giant backpack. We think we pay attention to our bodies by pumping and pummelling them in the gym to make them tighter, by sticking in implants or 'liposucking' them, but to relate to our body as a part of us isn't usually on the agenda. Mostly, we use our body as bait to haul in a mate.

We pride ourselves on pushing ourselves to our limits and beyond. This is why you hear people say, 'I shopped till I dropped'; 'I've done all my Christmas cards and it's only July'; 'I lost 100lbs in one week. Now I'm on life-support, but I am a size six.'

I once saw a physical-fitness trainer turn up at the gym kitted out in a back brace, as if it was some kind of war wound and he was awarded it for an act of bravery. He'd disjointed every one of his spinal discs, or something, in order to stay bulked up, with no awareness that the injury, too, was something he had done to himself. What did he think had happened? That a meteorite fell from the sky and caused the injury? You hear screams of agony coming out of the gym as if some of these men have just given birth through their nostrils.

I have a friend who, in the name of yoga, used to tie her feet in a bow above her head. She proudly told me that she has had to have her hips replaced . . . because that's how flexible she is.

Mindful movement is about becoming aware of your bodily senses in so far as they are reflections of your thoughts. If your body is tight and rigid, your thoughts are probably also inflexible. If your spine is held in a hunched-over posture and your shoulders are up to your ears, you could be locked in a state of anger or fear. In addition to these feelings, we can become angry at our bodies for not doing what we want them to do, and when the kick-in-the-face realization dawns on us that our body will eventually fall to bits anyway, no matter how much we did on the StairMaster. Then, as our body starts to lose its tone and its strength, we push it harder and harder, punishing it for letting us down rather than thanking it for the ride so far. (By the way, I haven't accomplished this: I'm still whipping myself into shape; as I type, I'm tightening my glutes.) Very few of us listen to what our body is trying to tell us, because we're lost in our thoughts. The body can be a fantastic barometer and show us how we are, not how we think we are.

Mindful movement tunes you into every part of your body, so that you pay attention to any tension or resistance and notice when the mind tries to take you away and create more tension with its endless bad reviews. ('Why am I feeling this? I want it to go away.' 'I'm just an iglooed mountain of lard. I'm useless.')

I notice that on the rare occasions when my body feels free (maybe after a strong massage, where someone has had to use a hammer to give me some relief from my solid, turtle-shell back) my mind is clearer, I'm less anxious and I become a bundle of joy to be around. When I spend the day in my usual Hunchback of Notre Dame, reptilian-rage position, with my shoulders up so high I can wear them as earmuffs, I'm a bitch. How you feel in your body is a physical manifestation of your thoughts, how you relate to your thoughts is how you relate to people, and how you react to people is how you react to the world. To focus into your body is like going on an internal retreat, away from the fascist dictator of your mind. So scanning your body for tension and then releasing it is a way of getting off your own back.

With practice, you will eventually be able to discern when you're working at your limit, pushing yourself hard enough to get results but not so hard that you're in agony. By building up your awareness of this physical limit, you can apply it to your life and push yourself just enough to work at your optimum. You will be tuned into your body, so when it's telling you there's too much pain, you'll hear it and pull back.

Please note that there are some people who go too far the other way, refusing to move or even attempt one sit-up (*see* couch potato), giving excuses like, 'I'm just naturally fat.' Have you ever seen an obese newborn? I don't think so. Your body, if you listen to it, will let you know when it needs to work harder and when it needs to lay off.

Before MBCT, Jon Kabat-Zinn, a molecular biologist and Emeritus Professor of Medicine at the University of Massachusetts Medical School, founded MBSR (Mindfulness-Based Stress Reduction). He worked with people who were in such chronic pain from injury or disease that their doctors couldn't help. He told his patients that, rather than repressing or ignoring the pain, they should send their focus to the precise area where they were experiencing discomfort. By focusing on the raw sensations (throbbing, pulsing, stabbing), the minds of his patients ceased their relentless catastrophizing and the patients began to notice that their pain wasn't a solid block. The sensations came and went, grew stronger and weaker . . . they were always transforming. Kabat-Zinn had enormous success with his patients: they still felt their pain, but their relationship to it changed and that made it manageable. Taking on board the idea that pain changes moment by moment is what liberated them from their prison of constant agony.

This week's exercises, as you would expect, are all about mindful movement. I'm giving you three options.

1. Normal mindful movement
2. Mindful movement in the gym (for people who can't stand mindful movement)

3. Mindful movement on the go (for people who can't even stand mindful movement in the gym)

The movements in all the exercises which follow will train you to use your body as an anchor, something to come back to when your mind starts to go frantic on you. The stretching will make your body feel less tense and caged in by your muscles. As you stretch, both the body and the mind free up, and this is not just a metaphor: as you move, more blood flows to your organs and more oxygen flows to the brain. Usually, if your body is rigid, so is your mind . . . unless of course you're Stephen Hawking, and then all the laws of logic go up the spout.

When practising mindful movement, do *not* do it: on a train; in a taxi; in a queue; in the waiting room of the dentist's office (unless you're alone); in a meeting room at work (if the walls are glass and people can see in). (I don't really care what people think, so I do it in all these places.)

Exercises: Normal Mindful Movement

Do these exercises for ten to twenty minutes each day for six days.

Head Roll

Stand with your feet slightly apart, your spine straight but not rigid, your shoulders relaxed and the crown of your head pointing to the sky. Now bring your focus to the top of your head and slowly let the weight of it pull you to the right, so that your right ear is pointing towards your right shoulder.

Let it hang there and notice the sensation. Are you straining to get your head lower to your shoulder, or allowing it to hang by its own weight? While your head's still in that position, scan your body for any other indication of strain. Now add the breath . . . Use the breath as if it's a beam of light, helping you find and investigate where the tension is. On the inhale, send your focus to the area of the stretch on the left side of your neck and, on the exhale, release it. As it's suspended, your mind might no longer be on the sensation itself but lost in a story. If you notice this is happening, send the focus back to the area where you feel the stretch. Now slowly, still focused on every movement, bring your head back to centre and move it towards your left shoulder. Using the in-breath, now bring your focus to the stretch on the right side of your neck, and release it on the out-breath. Bring it up to the centre and notice what effect the exercise has had. Now let go of the focus . . . Repeat twice on each side.

Shoulder Roll

Bring your attention to both your shoulders. Lift them both and circle them slowly forwards five times. Try to stay with every sensation of the movement. Notice when you're making too much of an effort, or if you're tensing any other part of your body. Let your shoulders simply drop at the lowest point of the circle rather than pushing them down. Inhale when you lift them up; when you circle them, exhale so the breath focuses your attention on the movement. Now do the same in the opposite direction; again, five times. Are you still breathing? Come back to neutral and become conscious of the effects the exercise has had. Let the focus go . . .

Side Stretch

Bring your attention to all the sensations in both of your arms as you raise them up above your head, palms facing each other. Feel the sensation of their weight as you raise them. Gradually, bend from your waist to the right, your arms parallel, either side of your head. Bend far enough so that you can feel the stretch but not beyond your limit. Notice if your mind has left the building and, if so, be nice and refocus on the stretch. Come back to upright, your arms still above your head, and lean your body to the left, feeling the pinch of your waist on the left and the long stretch along the right. Come back to upright again and lower your arms to your sides. Feel the effects of the stretch and release your focus. Repeat twice on each side.

Body Roll

Stand up straight, with your head up and your legs hip-width apart. On an exhale, slowly curve forward, letting your head lead and feeling the weight of it pulling you down, vertebra by vertebra (keep breathing) until you're hanging at the bottom, allowing gravity to take over. Even if you've just moved an inch, don't push; the point is to be aware of what's happening in your body and mind. On another exhale, unroll, bringing up your spine, vertebra by vertebra, as if you were stacking up dominoes. Stand very straight, until your head feels balanced on top of your spine. Feel the effects of this exercise. Repeat.

The Cat

Get on all fours, your shoulders over your hands and your hips above your knees. Now, slowly, on an exhale, arch your spine up so it's humped like an angry cat and on the inhale bend your back the other way, raising your head and your bottom in the air. Repeat three times.

Curl Downs

Sit on the ground with both legs together in front of you, and curl your head forward towards your knees. Again, it's all about noticing what's going on, not about how far you can bend, so even if you move only a hair's breadth, don't push yourself. Try to stay in the position you've reached, inhaling and exhaling, sending focus to any area that aches or seems to be feeling any strain. Notice whether, while you're in this position, anything changes. Repeat twice.

Hip Roll

Now lie on the ground on your back with your legs and your feet together and bent in an 'L' shape, your feet in the air. Stretch your arms flat on the floor at right angles to your body. As you inhale, bring both legs, still together and bent, towards the floor to the right, sensing each part of the movement and using your abdominal muscles for stability. Go as far as you can, noticing the stretch and breathing into your left side. On the exhalation, bring the legs back to the centre and, on an inhalation, slowly move them to left, feeling the stretch on your right side. On an exhale, bring them back to the centre.

If you have any problems with your back, keep your feet on the floor and let your knees tilt to either side as far as they can, with your feet and ankles following. In this position you can turn your head the opposite way to your body to give an extra stretch. Repeat twice on each side.

Exercises: Mindful Movement in the Gym (for people who can't stand mindful movement)

When you're walking, running, swimming, sitting in front of the computer or partying, scan your body for any area that's tense and breathe into it. Remember: every time you send focus to a sense in your body, you're not slacking, you're strengthening the parts of your brain that enhance self-regulation. Even if you do this only for a minute a day, it gets results. Go look in a brain scanner if you have one handy.

There will be those of you who find the Mindful Movements too boring even to discuss and too slow to tolerate, but you, too, can be mindful: during your regular exercise regime. If you want to pump it like a maniac wearing an 'I ROCK' baseball cap while some trainer the size of the Hulk barks, 'Crunch it till you cry, I want you bleeding from your ears! No pain, no gain!' If you're paying attention to the area you're exercising, you'll still see better results than if you were mind-wandering. New neurons will not grow in the region of your brain that corresponds to the area you're exercising unless you're focused on those particular parts of your body. If a piano player isn't focused on their fingers, they'll never master the piano. So, whatever you're pumping, pulling, sucking in or flexing, be aware of it. If you're just doing it on automatic, you may end up looking like some over-buffed gorilla in a neck brace.

Here are some suggestions for some fast and furious exercises.

On an Exercise Bike or a Running Machine

Exercise for however long you usually exercise, but try these, each for around twenty seconds (use the timer on the equipment, or try counting for twenty breaths).

While you are cycling or running, send your attention to your feet, specifically the points at which they contact the pedals or the running belt. Feel each movement, and breathe. After twenty seconds, let the focus go . . .

If you're on a bicycle, bring your attention to your pelvic area wherever it makes contact with the seat and to your hips and waist. (In other words, the area that would be covered if you were wearing full-sized underpants.) Breathe into all the sensations you are experiencing in these areas. Notice if your mind wanders, and if it does be nice to yourself and refocus on that under-pant terrain. If you're running, focus on the same region for twenty seconds. Then let the sensation go . . .

Now, for twenty seconds, shift your focus first to the bottom of your spine then all the way up to your shoulders. What does your posture feel like from the inside? Are you hunched or tensed? Are your shoulders back or forward? Notice it, but don't change it. Let it go . . .

Then, for twenty seconds, feel the sensation of your hands on the handlebars, or just the sensation in your hands. Are they gripping tightly, limp or numb? Watch when your mind carries you away and bring it back to your hands. Let it go . . .

Bring your attention to your neck and face. Is your neck forward, back, held or balanced? Scan your facial features: chin, jaw, lips, tongue, nose, forehead, scalp. What expression are you wearing on your face? Do you look like a gargoyle? Again, do this for twenty seconds.

Finally, for twenty seconds, bring your focus to your whole body from your feet, up through your body, to the top of your head; fill up like a balloon on the inhale and empty on the exhale. Let it go . . .

If you find yourself unable to focus on any of these areas, the most important thing is not to give yourself a hard time. Go back to doing what you usually do on the bike. If you need to distract yourself by watching MTV, listening on your headphones or perusing *Heat* magazine, go ahead. If you notice you're doing it, then it's mindful – even if you're mindfully watching MTV.

Arm Curls with Weights

Place a hand-weight (of the weight you usually work with) or a tin of beans (or whatever) in your right hand. Start with your arm falling straight by your side and then, on an exhale, bend it at the elbow and bring the weight up to shoulder height. On an inhale, lower your arm to your side. Try to pay attention to where any twinges may be, scanning your body to check if you're tensing any other part of it which isn't involved in the curl. Repeat ten times on each arm. If that's too hard, reduce to five.

Tricep Curls

Hold a weight in your right hand then lift your arm so it is pointing straight up beside your head. On an inhale, bend your elbow and lower the weight behind your back (as if you were reaching to scratching between your shoulder blades. On an exhale, lift the arm up again. Repeat ten times on each arm and, as you become more proficient, build up the number.

Stomach Crunches

Lie on your back with your legs bent and your feet on the floor about hip-width apart. Put both hands behind your head and, on an exhale, pull in your abdomen as if you've been punched and curl your upper body forward (without jerking yourself up by your neck). Scan your body to make sure you're just using your stomach muscles and nothing else. On an inhale, uncurl down to the floor. Repeat five to ten times.

Bottom Crunches

Lie on your back with your legs bent and your feet on the ground about hip-width apart. On an exhale, tighten your bottom and lift it so that your back arches, your navel pointing to the sky. Hold the position, still clenching your bottom and feeling the slight ache (not agony) in the back of your thighs, then lay your back down again. There you have it: you're getting a tight bum while being mindful. Repeat five times.

Homework

Note any observations on the exercises you have done in your diary.

Here are some questions to have in your mind.

- How were the exercises different when you started to practise mindfulness while doing them?
- When your mind wandered, did you recall any of the thoughts you had?
- When you held a position, what, if any, changes did you notice?

Again, this week, try to do the three-minute mindfulness breathing exercise twice a day, either when you notice that your thoughts are scattered and you're becoming anxious, or simply to get back into the present.

Exercises: Mindful Movement on the Go (for people who can't even stand mindful movement in the gym)

Street Curls

You don't go to a gym or do any exercise? This works for me. You know when you're carrying a couple of heavy bags and feel like your arms are being yanked out of your armpits? Bitching about it won't help; it will only make you more frustrated. Why not try – as you have to carry the bags anyway – to make use of the time not just to get mindful but also to build up some muscles? As you're walking, even if you are in a hurry, lift the bag in your right hand up towards your shoulder and hold for a count of ten. Just as you would with a weight, focus into the area where you feel the ache and breathe into it. On the street, it's crucial to do a body scan for tension, because we're used to lifting our shoulders up or tensing our bodies when we carry something heavy. (Why some of us are happy to lift weights in the gym but don't make the most of it outside with heavy bags I do not know.) Now repeat with your left arm.

Bag Lifts

I also do tricep curls in public on the street, because I really don't really care what people think of me and usually people don't notice anything anyway. You raise and straighten one arm, holding a bag beside your head, then bend your arm and lower the bag behind your back. Lift the bag and straighten your arm for a count of ten. Repeat on the other arm. Be aware of all the sensations you're experiencing and, if your mind goes on holiday, bring it back.

Trolley Pumping

Pushing a shopping trolley is good for strengthening and stretching your arms. Pull the trolley towards you (it's better if there's a lot of merchandise in it), your hands clutching the bar as they normally would, then push it away and pull it back to you ten times. (Don't tense your shoulders, just use your arms, or you'll get the vulture wings my mother had.) Now hold the bar of the trolley but with your palms facing up, and repeat.

Trolley Stretching

Hold the bar of the trolley and allow the trolley to roll forward so your back gets a long stretch, parallel to the ground. (If you're still in the supermarket, pretend you've dropped something and you're looking for it on the floor.) Stand upright again. Repeat five times.

Working with Luggage

Are you at the airport or the train station, and late? Even if you are, don't tense up while you're running to make that plane or train. Focus on where your feet make contact with the floor to stop your thoughts getting at you with, 'You idiot, you're late again! This is all your fault – you were taking a bath when the taxi pulled up. Typical.' Straighten your body, relax your shoulders and take the leash attached to your wheelie. Pull it towards you then push it away again. Repeat this ten times. This bulks up your biceps mindfully and you still make it to the plane or train.

(You could try this while walking a large dog, but I wouldn't recommend it: you might accidentally choke it.)

Elevator

An elevator is the perfect vehicle in which to stretch out your body. Put your foot on the handrail (if you can) and bend towards it, stretching the back of your standing leg. Repeat on the other leg. Next, standing, bend one leg backwards and grab your ankle behind you, stretching those thighs. Repeat on the other leg. If you're going up to the top of the Empire State or the Shard, you'll have time to continue, by lying on the floor and lifting one leg at a time in a leg stretch. You could even try a backbend. Really, you can do pretty much anything in a lift. And if someone else is there too, ignore them, because you're getting fit and they aren't.

Stretching at the Luggage Carousel. Or Wherever

Use your time effectively when you're waiting for your luggage to show up (or in any queue). Rather than shouting or becoming inwardly furious (it won't get your luggage there any quicker or move the queue any faster, you know), take the opportunity to do a neck stretch, a shoulder roll and a side stretch. Still waiting? Try the backbend. If you're doing these exercises with awareness rather than looking around you in embarrassment, you're being mindful.

Shoulder-bag Stretches

For anyone carrying a shoulder bag . . . Put the strap over one of your shoulders, then lean your head over the other shoulder so you feel a great stretch along your neck and, if you lean deeper into it, your waist. Remember to change shoulders, or you'll find that you're lopsided.

WEEK FOUR:
Mindfulness of Feelings and Emotions

Just as we've sent the focus of our attention to our feet, our seat, to sounds, the body and breathing, now we're going to send it to where we feel emotions in the body. The process is exactly the same: you can feel an ache of emotion in your body as much as you can feel an ache or a strain during a physical stretch in an exercise. In both cases, the idea is to move towards the feeling, not run from it. If you think, 'I don't want these feelings, I want them to go away,' they will attack you harder and stick around longer.

Cocktails of chemicals are constantly cascading through your veins, creating feelings and emotions; you'll never fathom out how this works, so just experience them and skip the interpretation. (Unless you're a poet, in which case, go for it.)

Pure awareness of a feeling (physical or emotional) allows you to go below negative self-talk and means that you don't have to pick the scab of memory. If you catch the feeling quickly and hone in on it, you'll nip the verbal translation in the bud. The idea is to contain the fire before it catches.

I revealed earlier that I am (but less so, these days) addicted to rage. Letting it rip used to be my favourite hobby. On a day out, I'd hunt down traffic wardens, wait for them behind a tree then jump out, crazier than a coot. They never tore up the parking ticket they'd given me, but my fury felt great, and fed my addiction. The next day, I'd have a hangover from the all bile I'd brought up.

Only when I became aware of my dangerous patterns of thinking and how they affected other people did I start to loosen the strings of my straitjacket. I realized that each time I had a hit of rage, I was hard-wiring and mainlining my habit even more.

Whenever I do any physical exercise, I notice that, in certain parts of my body, I feel a familiar ache. Even if I do temporarily get rid of it, the next day it's back again, in the same place. I've learnt to live with it, treating my pains like old friends. I wake up going, 'Hello, there's the old knee pain. How ya doin'?' 'Yup, there it is, my cramping neck, doing its thing. Howdy!' It's the same with emotions: I'm learning to recognize the familiar ones as they arise and greet them with, 'Hi there, ache in my heart, didn't I have you yesterday . . . and the day before . . . and most of my life? Welcome back.' We all have certain emotions that repeat themselves again and again: our emotional theme tunes.

Just by accepting what's there without pushing it away, complaining about it or denying it, the feelings will transform in intensity, perception or location. When they become too acute, take the focus back to your breath or directly to the raw feelings. When you're ready, come back to the sense of breathing.

Exercise: Mindful Emotions

Practise for five to ten minutes.

Remember: you can sit anywhere for these exercises, or, if you really hate sitting, do it in any position, anywhere. If you happen to be sitting ... come forward with your back straight and the crown of your head pointing to the sky and bring your focus to both feet. Let that go and bring your attention to your breath, not forcing it but allowing it to happen on its own. (If it's easier, count ten breaths.) Now widen your focus so that you are open to any emotional sensation in your body that might be pulling on your attention. When you've located the area, zoom in and investigate it with curiosity, not criticism. What shape is it? Is it pulsing, throbbing, stabbing or tickling?

Exercise: Dealing with the Difficult

You can continue this exercise on from the exercise above, or use it as a separate one. Practise for five to ten minutes.

As you're sitting there, focusing on your breathing, bring to mind a difficult situation that's either going on in your life at the moment or was in the past, a situation when you felt angry, resentful, anxious, stressed – anything that still has a small sting. Be aware that you're not bringing up these negative feelings in order to hurt yourself but to acknowledge and befriend the darker feelings that exist ... that are there anyway, even if you're not conscious of them. Turn to them with compassion and care, as you would to a friend who is suffering. And, once you've recognized the feeling, zoom in on where it is and use it as an anchor. Just before you finish, imagine a good experience which you've had in the past and see if your emotions resonate with the positive memory. Notice that you can influence your emotions by switching to more positive images in your mind; if the emotion gets too hot, refocus on a positive one. For the last few moments, bring your point of focus back to your breath, back to where you feel more peaceful and present.

Keep a diary over the next six days, jotting down your mindful feelings.

Here are a few questions to have in your mind.

- What emotion did you bring to mind in the exercise?
- Draw a picture of a body and illustrate where the feeling was. What colour was it? Shape? Size?
- Draw another picture of the body and illustrate what, if anything, changed during the exercise.

Again, this week, try doing the three-minute mindfulness breathing exercise twice a day.

WEEK FIVE:
Mindfulness of Thought

Just as with emotions, your thoughts can become habit-forming and obsessive. At times, they can be a waste of head space; at other times, they're a tiny bit useful because they give us poetry, art, literature, language, communication, civilization . . . to name a few. I'll keep saying it: when they're good, they're very, very good; and when they're bad they're evil. Our mission is to pick and choose to use them, and not to have them use us. So it's back to mindfulness, which is all about shifting the paradigm of your relationship to your thoughts: learning to sit back and choose when to grab a thought and when to let it go.

If you're observing your thoughts with a clearer, more settled mind, it goes without saying that some gems might arise from the darkness in the form of a great/ funny/ creative/ original thought.

Sometimes when I'm practising mindfulness, a fantastic idea bubbles out of the darkness to the surface and I sit there like an insane person, laughing out loud. As soon as I'm done, I grab a pen to get it down fast before it sinks back into the murk. Mindfulness isn't about sitting like a dead, frozen fish, you're there observing your thoughts, and with time it should become easier to discriminate between which thoughts are winners and which are dross to be flushed out on arrival. It's said that most creative thinking takes place when you're not striving for it; this is why people have epiphanies in the shower. It's probably similar for people who pan for gold; suddenly, they notice something sparkling there in the mud. This is how it feels when I occasionally notice a great line lying there in the murk.

Be Your Own Therapist

In the same way that you deal with hot emotions by standing back from them, you can learn to detach from your thoughts. With mindfulness, you're the therapist to yourself, listening to your own deep, dark thoughts. Just like the shrink, who doesn't bring any judgement to the table, your mind, if it's not threatened or fearful, will reveal to you who you are, and then you can unchain yourself from those limiting, destructive thoughts and create new ones. If you don't look in and become aware, you'll be trapped in habits and keep playing the same old tune, like a needle that's stuck in the groove of a record.

Exercise: Mindful Thinking

Practise for ten minutes every day for the next six days.

Sit on a chair or a cushion and bring your back upright, unsupported, your head balanced on top of your spine. Sense both feet flat on the ground and the weight of your body on the seat, and bring your focus to your breath (counting to ten with each breath, if it's easier). Notice when your mind wanders and bring your focus back to that pinpoint of breathing. Expand your awareness to sound; just listen, letting the sound come to you without hunting for it.

Now bring your attention to your thinking, watching whatever comes up, just as you let the sounds come to you. If you like, imagine these thoughts as clouds continuously moving across the sky; some are heavy, some light, some thunderous, but they keep moving and transforming without any effort on your part. If this doesn't work for you, imagine that you're sitting in a cinema watching a film and, up on the screen, your thoughts are coming out of the mouths of different characters. You're just sitting, watching, maybe eating popcorn or a hot dog. You might notice at some point that you've left your seat, joined the film and become part of the plot. As soon as you realize this has happened, without giving yourself a bad review, walk back to your seat, pick up the popcorn and watch again. Whether the film is hilarious or terrifying, just watch from your seat and notice whenever you're up there on the screen. You don't get a better score the fewer times you move to the screen and back; the point is to notice each time you do. If you do it a hundred times, pat yourself on the back and congratulate yourself for being aware that you did. As I said in Chapter 2, it's actually a better mental exercise when you mind-wander and then bring your focus back, because each time you do it beefs up those mental abs. In the last few moments of the exercise, come back to simply breathing; each time you remember to breathe or sit back in your chair in the cinema, you're automatically in the present. The breath is always there for you to bring you back to a sense of peace and presence.

Write your thoughts after each meditation in your diary each day.

Here are some questions to have in your mind.

- How did it feel when you shifted from listening to sounds to listening to your thoughts?
- Using the cloud or cinema image, what were your thoughts when your mind wandered? Are there any themes?
- How did you respond when you realized (if you did) that you had become part of the film and needed to return to your seat?
- Was the popcorn good?

WEEK SIX:
Overview: Putting It All Together

This week, you are going to work on how to incorporate mindfulness into your real life. That's the point of it (not to learn to be a log).

You can't be present all the time, watching your feelings and thoughts, or you'd grind to a halt, maybe mid-walk or, even worse, mid-traffic. My hunch is that only yogis who live in caves or people with specific types of brain damage experience that state of being permanently present.

A Day in the Life of a Working Person

7 a.m. Alarm clock goes off. *Try, try, try* to set the clock ten minutes earlier so you might have time do a five- to ten-minute mindfulness session (choose any exercise from my six-week course) or, if there's simply no time, just have your shower or brush your teeth with awareness. If you don't have time to brush your teeth, see a doctor . . . and a dentist.

8 a.m. If you have time while you're getting ready for work to throw some coffee, tea or even food into your mouth, maybe for two or three bites you can experience the temperature, flavour, size or taste of what you're eating/ drinking, the flavour, size and taste? (Remember: even a few seconds makes a difference in your brain.)

8.30 a.m. Get in the car and drive (if you drive to work). At this point, don't even think about focusing on your senses or coming into the present, because you'll have an accident and I don't want to be blamed. Most of the time we have to be on automatic pilot; this is one of those times.

However, if you're taking a bus, train, taxi or horse, this is a good time to do some mindfulness practice. Do any of the following: feel your feet on the ground, feel your body on the seat, listen to sound, focus on your breath, watch yourself thinking and, if you're getting jumpy because you're going to be late, focus on the feeling of jumpiness.

9 a.m.–1 p.m. Any time during the morning, if you notice yourself getting a brain-clog or a red mist coming down, do a three- or even one-minute mindfulness exercise, at your desk, under your desk, in the elevator, in the loo . . . Try doing it twice a day – maybe once before lunch, and once after. If you close the lid of your laptop, turn off your phone or just walk away for those three minutes/ one minute, I promise, when you resume your work, you'll be clearer, more creative, more energized and you'll beat the competition as they burn out around you.

1 p.m. Lunchtime. Wherever you're eating, taste the food while you're chewing and swallowing it, if only for a few seconds; otherwise, it's a waste of money and calories. If you have to eat lunch in a meeting, still make the effort to taste the food . . . no one else will notice and, at the same time, you'll be clearing head space by sending your focus to the 'eats' department.

4 p.m. Usually, it's towards the end of the day that most of us get tired, but that's exactly when I start gunning my engine, wheels spinning, to get the job done. I'm not getting anywhere, though, because, mentally, I've run out of fuel, even though I'm still jamming my foot to the floor. It's so sad, but it's my syndrome, my addiction to adrenaline, which I pump up with 'last minutism'. I drive myself to the

edge of the cliff and hang there, exhausted. But while I'm dangling over the chasm by my fingernails, it would help to take a one- or three-minute mindfulness pause.

7 p.m. You're now going to need a whole new set of gears for what's called your home life. I'd suggest before you see your family you do a little mindfulness practice so you don't bring any of the dross home from work. Maybe for a minute listen to sound; you don't even need to switch on music, just listen to ambient noise to come back to your senses and out of your head. (And I don't mean by getting loaded on the way home.) You're now attempting to transform yourself from the work-mode you to the person who talks to people and listens to them.

8 p.m. and onwards. If you've been practising MBCT regularly, it will become easier to switch off from your working day in the company of your family and friends. If you notice that your mind is still at the office, overthinking, take your focus to noticing the people around you. You can put that amygdala away, you won't be needing it now; there is no danger among friends and family . . . unless, of course, you're Macbeth.

11 p.m. In bed, if you can try a three-minute practice, it might help you to fall asleep more quickly. Just lie there and allow your thoughts to have one last orgy: ruminate, worry, plan, fantasize, brood, let rip. After a minute, bring your focus back to your breath and, in the last minute, breathe into your body from your toes to your head. zzzzz

Throughout your day, there are specific times when mindfulness might come in handy.

At the Bus Stop

Your bus is late, you're late, and now you've turned into the Alien, full fangs exposed, saliva dripping. Looking at your watch furiously won't make the bus come any faster. If you've been practising mindfulness regularly, it might not be so difficult to become aware that you've lost your mind. I know: it's horrifying to get a glimpse of the idiot you're making of yourself, screaming like a crazy person to no effect – other than to be filmed by someone nearby who will upload the video on to YouTube.

Speaking in Public

If ever you are called upon to do some public speaking, here's a tip. Now, I know this sounds weird, but go into the loo, lock the door and just sit there on the seat (lid up or down), focusing on the sensations you feel. If you start to think how weird the situation is, take your focus to the seat.

On your way to speak, send your focus to where your feet contact the ground. If you get nervous, as you're speaking, you can also intermittently throw some focus to your feet, literally, to ground yourself.

Morning Mindfulness

Most mornings I wake up mentally clogged from the nocturnal orgy of imaginings left over from the night before. (Sometimes, at the end of my dreams, the credits run by – they're usually Polish names.) If I don't practise mindfulness for even ten minutes in the morning, I know they'll stay in my head and infect the rest of my day. To me, practising every morning is exactly like using the loo, in that, if you don't evacuate what's in you, you'll feel discomfort all day long. My theory is that dreams are the same: you need to have some kind of exit strategy for them, or they'll just sink into your unconscious and eventually blow out of you. So each morning I patiently sit on my bed and allow the dreams into my consciousness and notice that, eventually, they lose their grip and their solidity. Here are a few examples of why my dreams need to be gently excavated.

My Dream

A few nights ago, I dreamt that Alan Rickman had just stabbed me in the roof of my mouth at a delicatessen, for no reason. I then went into a Zara shop in India, asked for a needle and thread and sewed the wound together, my mouth wide open like a lion's. I then tied the thread into a big bow. (The dream continues in this vein . . .)

I've left my car in a no-parking zone and, when I return, I notice it's been completely dismantled; only the chassis is left. The guy (gangster) who tore it apart tells me he'll put it together again if I pay him $5,000. I refuse, so he takes me to his leader, who looks like Idi Amin. I try to make Idi laugh by showing him how I can turn his porno photos into key chains. He laughs maniacally, and I think, 'Sucker, I got him, I won't have to pay the $5,000.' As I'm leaving, a group of Vietnamese boy-soldiers marches by and Idi hacks off the head of one of them with a jousting stick and tells me that if I don't pay the $5,000 that will happen to me. I decide to get the money. I jump into a white stretch limo and spend the night going from cashpoint to cashpoint collecting it; I decide I'll pay him back in avocados. Jump cut: I'm working around the clock with Chinese workers, wrapping up thousands of avocados ... Do you see now why, sometimes, I wake up feeling anxious?

6

The Social Mind: Mindful Relationships

Underneath our hairless skin, we (humans) are social animals; whether we like it or not, or whether we like each other or not, we continue to exist only through our relationships. Language, art, civilization and religion all grew out of a need to connect. If we were all isolated, we wouldn't have made it this far (certainly not without Tinder). Also, you can't gossip when you're alone; it won't work, I've tried.

> You: Do you know what I did last night?
> You: I was alone and didn't meet anyone.
> You: What were you wearing?
> You: Oh, the same old buffalo skin over-the-shoulder one-piece.
> You: Who designed it?
> You: Me.

The brain itself is a social organ; on its own, it's just a 3lb piece of jelly. It only comes to life when it mingles with other brains; it's then that the party starts. The brain is organized through social interaction and by engagement with other minds; it's wired to connect right from the start. Even in the womb, the baby's brain and body are influenced by the environment. Is the amniotic fluid warm enough? Is the womb too small? How is it decorated? Is there too much bling in there? Once out in the fresh air, if there isn't the necessary parent or caregiver on hand to shape and develop the baby's brain, things could get sticky – literally, because who's going to change the nappy? And without the feedback of facial expressions, reciprocal 'goo-goo'-ing and exchange of the bonding hormone, oxytocin, the child might grow up to find themselves playing a lifetime of solitaire. Just about everything that makes us human – our ability to speak, to think, to love and to hate – depends on our relations to each other.

Relationships weren't my speciality (especially when I was young) as far as the opposite sex was concerned. I might be missing some crucial hormone, because no one but the really creepy guys in high school has ever tried to pick me up. In school, all the good-looking boys would throw the really pretty girls in the lake, and they'd scream, 'Don't throw me in! Don't throw me in!' I screamed, 'Don't throw me in!' and no one ever did. And it wasn't just that men were rejecting me. I was always left out in school gangs, too. All the popular girls could smell that I was not of their species and come over to me, saying things like, 'Do you look like that on purpose?' I only found my people when I was insti-tutionalized; I felt understood and safe even with the ones who set their hair on fire and claimed that Norman the Con-queror was passing them secrets.

You can go to the zoo and watch our not-so-distant cousins, the apes, working naturally as a unit: bonding, playing, eat-ing and mating with each other. Luckily, we don't have to pick nits out of each other's hair or be constantly hit on by the alpha-ape, because we have relationship counsellors to advise us on better ways of communicating. We're able to attune to each other by allowing our own internal states to resonate with the inner world of the person we are talking to, so that when two people are interacting, the same brain structures are active; it's a kind of dance of mutual responsiveness. This is why you see everyone cry or laugh at the same time when they're watching a film. If you don't believe me, just sit in the front row for *Toy Story*, turn around and watch what happens when Jesse sings 'When She Loved Me'. (I had to be carried out by paramedics. I lost 200lbs in mucus and tears.) Whichever way you look at it, we are all in this together.

We pass our moods and emotional states on to each other like a virus. Don't think you can hide your mood; the other person may not know exactly what you're thinking but they can pick up what state you're in loud and clear. Everyone knows 'passive aggressive' when they see it (smiling with fangs out), so you're not fooling anyone. We work like neural Wi-Fi; whatever I'm feeling, I'll pass to you, and that passes to whomever you meet and ripples out to your friends, workmates, neighbours, community, town, country . . . planet. You smile, the world smiles with you. (That's not completely true, but you get what I mean . . .) You can't change the world by howling to the gods or by hurling money or missiles at the problem. However, by becoming aware of your inner state, you won't spend your life blaming the enemy; it may just lurk within.

So how did we turn into what we are now? What's gone wrong and what's gone right?

A Brief History of Human Relationships

Paul Gilbert, Professor of Clinical Psychology at the University of Derby, is an expert on the social brain and the nature of compassion, and I advise you to read his books (after you finish mine, of course). He reminds us that, in our early days, we were part of small, isolated groups of about a hundred or two hundred people, all genetically linked. We all knew each other (and, I'm sure, had sex with each other). Survival depended on sharing and caring, even though certain inbred mutations came with the package (*see* Alabama). The good news was that everyone was family and everyone cared about each other's welfare. If you went out hunting (not me; I've said this before: I come from a tribe that doesn't hunt; we point at what we want) and you didn't come back, people in your clan would go out to look for you. To this day, we still all want to feel that, if we suddenly disappeared, others would look for us and we wouldn't be forgotten.

Think of those films where they all go to the planet of Klingfilmium and Sigourney Weaver (or a younger version), in khaki army pants and string bikini top, goes back five thousand years in time with a crew of manly hunks to rescue some guy whose spaceship ran out of gas and who's been frozen in an ice bucket all this time, waiting for the space version of the AA to pick him up and defrost him. The whole cinema audience cheers when Sigourney (or a younger version) kisses him, and they return to Earth to live a boring life.

Anyway, what happened next was that the tribes expanded into cities and cities turned into shopping malls and we stopped caring about each other. (So if we lost our partner/toddler in Zara, we'd never think of going back to find them.

Or is this just me?) And, as we populated the planet and needed to find ways to communicate to a wider audience, enter the internet. This was probably around the time we started to lose some of our interpersonal skills and became more and more isolated behind our screens. (The truth is, Facebook doesn't cut it. We need to be skin to skin to really go under the radar of words and catch each other's drift.) This is why companies have to hire motivational speakers to teach some of the most powerful people in the world skills such as rapport, trust and compassion. Sad to realize that these aren't attributes people assume you'd need as you climb up the ladder of success.

These days, we sometimes delude ourselves that we're fighting for things like justice or world peace but, in my (often brutal) opinion, we're simply appeasing our primitive urge to let it rip on some random foe – any foe, irrespective of race, religion or political affinity. We all carry the seeds of bigotry, tribalism, greed and selfishness, and we should be aware that, as civilized as we think we are, we were the ones who both built the Colosseum and put on floor shows that make *The Hunger Games* seem like miniature golf. We don't need to cultivate negative behaviour; nature gives it to us for free.

We have to come to grips with the fact that, underneath our mild-mannered outsides, inside, we're still (how can I put this delicately?) wild animals (especially my parents and me). I don't care what kind of car you drive or how designer your label, below that snazzy front you're still living in the bush. You're not even potty-trained.

It takes great courage to stand apart from your politically or religiously motivated tribe and think about humanity as a whole. That's the true nature of compassion: not just thinking about your own kind but all kinds of people. This, again, is about being able to tolerate the different aspects of yourself, to tolerate differences in other people, and it's how we cultivate empathy. Yes, there is hope that we can break out of our cocoon of self-absorption. It's inbuilt in us, every mammal has it (lizards couldn't give a damn), but because we're living in a selfish world it's a little rusty and out of commission. You can even see evidence in an MRI scanner that certain areas in the brain become active when they respond to kindness and compassion from another person, and the corresponding areas in that other person are also active.

Professor Richard Davidson writes: 'We can intentionally shape the direction of plasticity changes in our brain. By focusing on wholesome thoughts, for example, and directing our intentions in those ways, we can potentially influence the plasticity of our brains and shape them in ways that can be beneficial. That leads us to the inevitable conclusion that qualities like warm-heartedness and well-being should best be regarded as skills.'

In 2014, I went to a retreat in New England led by Jack Kornfield, a doctor of clinical psychology who trained to become a Buddhist monk in Thailand, Myanmar and India. As you can imagine, he's kind of a heavyweight in the world of meditation.

Usually, when I get to any kind of large gathering and I'm alone, the first thing I do is to collect people to form my own gang. They're usually the spikier people there: the bitchy, funny and most cynical; of course, if there's anyone gay, I scoop them up too. But here there was a 'no talking' policy, so what would be the point of me hunting for my people?

There was a lot of hugging, which always creeps me out and makes me want to head for the hills, but as long as I didn't personally have to hug I was fine. As time went on I grew to love the silence: such a relief not have to indulge in small talk and act like you're fascinated by the mundane. If you don't talk, you can sit, surrounded by people with your own thoughts, watching the snow fall on the evergreen trees like on an American greeting card.

Jack Kornfield is the 'real deal'. He's completely present and calm, yet funny and razor sharp. He taught us a form of mindfulness which I practise only very occasionally . . . it's called mindful compassion. My cynical hackles were up, I was ready to pounce, but the exercise he taught us wiped the smirk right off my face. He asked us to pick a random partner and then for each of us to stare into our partner's eyes and imagine the other person as a child when they were laughing, in pain, etc. Then he had us imagine the other person as an adult, and experience their successes, their failures, difficulties and joy. I'd never met the woman who was my partner, but by the end of the exercise I felt I knew her better than I know some of my friends. It was so intimate, but she made me feel I was in safe hands. I stopped thinking about how she saw me; I just focused into her eyes, which showed every emotion under the sun. It seemed that an emotional bridge connected us; rather than us being two separate entities, our hearts and minds met somewhere in the middle. When we had finished, Jack said that what we had just experienced was compassion – but he didn't have to explain it; we felt it.

Before I left, I realized I loved all those braless Earth Mothers in their Uggs, and indeed I found myself hugging several of them. Thank God no photos were allowed.

So, although we come with savage tendencies, we also come with more virtuous qualities: peace, fairness, care, nurture and equanimity. Basically, we're a nice guy. The thing is, we don't bring these qualities out on show too often, just in case we get caught or pillaged with our pants down.

For every five of our negative thoughts, we have on average one positive thought, so we have at least got it in us. (One is better than none, I always say . . . it's not interesting, but I say it anyway.)

Even when you're alone, if you imagine being kind or compassionate, the same areas of your brain are as active as they would be if you were actively being kind. A similar mechanism causes us to catch each other's yawns by reciprocally activating the yawn area in each other's brain.

It's good to get to know our multidimensional selves; otherwise, we wouldn't be able to recognize other people as being anything other than two-dimensional stereotypes. Maybe the reason we do see people less fully than they actually are is because we want to feel safe; it's easier to label ourselves and other people as, for example, 'friendly', 'hostile' or 'shy'. In actual fact, we're all of these things; it's just that if we're not conscious of this, we will continue to believe our own inner CV: 'I'm a . . . (fill in your own) type of person.'

I hope you saw the brilliant, inspirational Disney film *Inside Out*. (I never thought I'd use those words together again once they'd given us Mickey and Donald Duck – the greatest philosophers of my generation.) It's about each of us being a potpourri of different personas, all of which are useful – even the asshole persona.

Mindfulness at Work

I think that the qualities of compassion and rapport are exactly what leaders of organizations need to get the best out of their staff and those they do business with. These days, people are required to work harder and longer hours and, recently, there's been a rise in absenteeism at work, partially due to stress-related disorders. So much is required from employees in terms of hitting targets; if they're going to function well in the future, corporations will need to switch their work modes from competition to cooperation. Maybe there should be some kind of reward which would reflect that ethos, so that if you help someone at work, it's noted and you get a bonus – anything from a new trophy wife/husband to a round of applause. The slogan of our times seems to be 'May the best man win, no matter how many heads have to roll.' Probably, if Macbeth were alive today, he would get into the Fortune 500 and be on the board of Goldman Sachs.

If we want our businesses – not to mention the human race – to succeed, we have to drop our obsession with 'me'-ness and start thinking more about 'we'-ness. We need to shift our eyes beyond personal greed to the bigger picture and see the ripple effects of our (and others') behaviour to kickstart us to act in new ways.

Leaders might have to learn that, before any meeting, they should take note of their inner state so as not to unconsciously pass their stress or aggression on to the next guy. If they learn to tolerate their feelings and not just fling them out, they can make everyone around them feel good and that they are heard. And if their mind is clear, they'll be able to listen rather than rant. That's how you succeed, not by pushing people to hit targets or meet bottom lines. Deep down, people don't really care about targets; they only really care if someone likes them or not.

It's true if we want to be a big success in whatever field we choose: we have to drop our obsession with 'me'-ness and start thinking more about 'we'-ness. When you're really listening to someone with curiosity, it's known as having rapport, which is the Dom Perignon of communication: it doesn't get better. If you give your full, fat attention to what someone is saying, it's the most flattering thing you can do to another human being and they'll either invite you home or adopt you. This goes back to my point about the importance of being able to pay attention: when a person is in front of you, you should not be thinking about a sandwich.

In this society, our survival depends on social acceptance and status, and we become stressed when we fall short in either of these areas. I have always fallen short.

I went to a garden party a few months ago and, this time, I was aware of why, in the past, I felt the need to get drunk. With so many people in one place, my mind was scattered to the wind, so I fell straight into my old habits from way back in childhood: getting people to laugh in order to gain their approval.

Why I need to do this I don't know. It could be that, when I was a child, I always thought that the more people I could get to like me, the more protected I would be from my parents' abuse. It was like building a human igloo of protection. Anyway, back to the party. I'm moving about like a starving animal, hunting from person to person for attention. I usually gravitate to the ones I perceive as the most powerful or the most popular. If I can get them to like me, my self-esteem goes up a mile. That feeling only lasts a few seconds, though, because it's such hard work. While I'm mentally tap-dancing for their attention, my mind is assaulting me with 'Any second they're going to find out that you're a fraud.'

There were famous people at this party, too. In the hierarchy of famous (even though I worked in television and may be considered famous by some), I am protoplasm. In these relationships it's implicit that I am the handmaiden who feeds them lines . . . and I know that's the deal, so no surprises. I'm ashamed to admit that, probably like other 'non-fames', when faced with an A-lister, I go into that slightly nervous, heart-pumping state of arousal, turning myself inside out to amuse. I'm sure it's a throwback to when I was a loser in high school; when the Prom Queen deigned to look at me I'd exhaust myself to get her approval. I never did. One of the great pleasures in my life now is knowing that said Prom Queen is ensconced in rehab.

Anyway, I spend the rest of the evening panicking about how long I'm supposed to talk to one person and when should I turn and talk to the next. (Is there an etiquette rulebook ? Why can't we do what we did as kids? Spit juice at the person and scream, 'You bore me!') I don't want the other person to turn away first – that would stab me in the heart – so I knock myself out trying to stay interested even if they're boring me senseless. I found myself saying to one guy, 'So tell me about the diggers you invest in over in East Africa.' I caught myself humped over, desperately trying to keep my interest going, but then I thought, 'I can't do this any more' and, making sure he didn't notice, I slipped away. I suppose that was being mindful, noticing that my mind was out of commission and that I wasn't really there, so I left and went to the loo to calm my racing mind. I could then clearly decide what I really felt I wanted to do. Without beating myself up about it, which is what would have happened five years ago, I went home to bed.

It turns out no one noticed I had left. Sometimes it's good not to feel like you have to steal the show – all you end up with is a hangover.

Some Suggestions for How to Deal with Relationships Mindfully

What to Do When Your Boss Tears Your Head Off

If you know that the meeting isn't going to be a bowl of cherries, prepare yourself. Breathe. Focus on the sounds. Look at a photo that brings back good memories and send your focus to your feet on the floor. Notice if you're starting to ruminate on a 'what-if' scenario and move your attention to where you feel the trepidation in your body. If your mind doesn't de-mist, don't berate yourself, just accept that that's where your mind is but recognize also that the noticing alone has done its thing on the cortisol overdrive.

When you come face to face with your boss and he/she is as confrontational as you feared, hold on to your hat.

What I do is to focus on the furious person's left eyebrow, or their right nostril (choose anything on the face near the eyes), and study it in minute detail: the hairs, the pores, the oils, the colour and how it changes. Your boss won't know you're not listening, because you're still looking in his direction. He'll want you to lob the anger ball back so he can give you another slam, but if you're grounded he can't play the game on his own and his anger will boomerang or peter out. Meanwhile, you've really learnt a lot about his nostril hair.

Alternatively, you can also choose to listen to your boss's anger as if it were the wind, with high and low notes, loud and soft. Don't focus on what he's saying, just the raw sounds emanating from his lips. This focus on sense keeps you out of word-slinging mode.

By using social intelligence (circumnavigating the blast

and not retaliating), you're showing not only compassion for yourself but compassion for your boss. You may still get fired, but you won't have given yourself a second dose of shame or pain.

How to Deal with Someone Who You Think is an Idiot

I have a weakness for this one. If I notice I want to eat someone alive and can catch myself early enough, I try to focus on their eyes and try to notice their fear rather than just treating them like a punch bag. If I can see the whites of their eyes and really spot the vulnerability, my compassion switches on. I am human, after all . . . sometimes.

How to Cope When Your Friend Cuts You Dead without Explanation

Notice your reactions and, whatever they are, that's okay, even if you do want to throw them under the wheels of a car or hide like a wounded animal. Hold back on your instinct to express your reactions straight away, either by bursting into tears or shouting like a fishwife/ husband. If you can sit and focus on the raw feelings, your mind will settle and you will come up with a more level-headed strategy in order to find out what's at the root of the problem without your old triggers blurring the picture. If your friend doesn't give you an answer, they weren't worth it anyway, but if they do tell you the truth, they're worth holding on to, because very few people do.

How to Deal with Your Partner, Who is Biting Your Head Off and It's Not Your Fault, It's His

When you notice that you're heading towards that old familiar duet of blame and finger-pointing performed in high C (one of my favourite tunes I sing to my husband is, 'Why are we going in the wrong direction? We're always lost! Why the fuck don't you ever use a map?'), try this (almost impossible) technique.

Keeping your tone even and low, say that you see your partner's point but you need to go to the loo; you'll be right back. (No one can ever argue if you need to go to the loo.) Go and sit in an enclosed space and try and focus on a few breaths. Even if you don't manage it, at least you took a pause, and a pause will give you both time to dump the adrenaline and rethink. I have never succeeded in this particular exercise, and I don't think anyone has.

I hope I haven't given the impression that mindfulness is just about sitting there in a chair, marinating in your own thoughts and loving yourself. The point of all this internal investigation is to become aware of the state you're in so that you don't infect anyone you come across by unconsciously dumping your mental trash on to them and then blaming them for your misery. No one said mindfulness was about letting people trample all over you or just accepting whatever, it's about making appropriate decisions for what's needed in specific situations. Sometimes you have to ease off; sometimes you have to put your foot on the pedal to kick everyone into action.

In conclusion, if we want to break our evolutionary ties with our beast within, we need to train ourselves to consciously move to our higher brain (before we tear the limbs off our opponent). At the same time, in doing this, we need to show some compassion for the beast within, because part of its actions got us this far. Without it, we would have been chewed up and spat out by now.

To evolve any further, we need to become conscious of these 'ancient whispers'. Underneath our mild-mannered exteriors lurk our barbaric brothers of the past and, if we are unaware of our own dark forces, they will act out by lobbing in a grenade when you least expect it.

In essence, it has taken us 4 billion years to evolve to where we are and, though we're cognitively brilliant, we're still a little emotionally dwarfed. The question is: can our more empathetic and compassionate side catch up? I say the first step is learning to hug your inner ape. (Perhaps the name of a new book? Or maybe not.)

My Entrée into a Relationship with the Human Race

To celebrate, before going to the silent retreat I visited in this chapter, I decided (randomly) to go to Bruges. I'd never been before, but I wanted to show my brain a good time for letting me use it as a repository for incoming research and an outgoing conduit to whatever it is you're now reading. (You be the judge of the contents, I'm just the messenger.) I wanted to go by myself to empty my mind, to be somewhere where there would be no associations that would spin my thoughts down Memory Lane. Distraction, when used discriminately and when it's appropriate, is a great braking system. This intentional act of closing down my own mother ship is a rare act of self-compassion. I wouldn't want to tip into burnout while writing a book on mindfulness – talk about shooting yourself in the foot.

As soon as I had sat on the train for a few hours (the first hour was hell; I spent it resisting the urge to jump off the train to go home and rewrite most of the book), the thoughts that were nagging at me to re-read the book became fainter. By the time I arrived in Bruges, those thoughts had all but vanished. If the city hadn't been filled with so much astounding eye candy, I might have been thinking, 'I shouldn't have come. I'm going to get lonely. Why Bruges?' But this place, miraculously, has been left untouched by time. Unlike any other city I've visited, it hasn't been Disneyized or filled with La Starbucks and Das McDonald's, cleverly integrated by some delusional city planner. I walked the narrow, cobbled streets lined with the original pointy-roofed houses (some accessorized with gold angels and saints), hearing myself say out loud, 'Oh my God!' I don't know how long I walked, gaping at everything, but I felt, because there was so little interference from upstairs, that I was taking whatever was there in 'eye-shot'. I was like an open lens. My 'to do' list was out of commission, my mental Wi-Fi was off and I felt human again. When I told a few friends I was going by myself, they thought it was strange and asked why I would do it. Now I can answer them. My concentration isn't split; I can stare at what I want for as long as I want without worrying about anybody with me, which I know is an old habit of mine. There isn't a moment of boredom as I watch the canal boats glide under the bridges, and admire those untouched seventeenth-century, moss-covered houses lining both sides of the canals.

Later that evening, I was still gawking and mumbling, 'Oh my God!', and I ended up in a town square packed to capacity with locals dancing to blasting salsa music. If I had been in pursuit of happiness, here it was. I stayed for hours, watching the pure joy on the dancers' faces as their feet, hips and arms moved in perfect synchronization. God, did I want to know how to salsa at that moment . . . badly. They were fully focused on what their bodies were doing, not at all on how they looked on the surface. There were old bald guys who looked eight months pregnant but who were doing magnificent footwork with nubile young women. Young guys were glued in a dancer's embrace to older women (some of them could have been my great-grandmother), occasionally tipping them into a back bend. Salsa is sexual, but they weren't using the dance as a pick-up ploy; they all seemed locked in the joy of mutual movement with whoever happened to be dancing in front of them. A woman in a wheelchair was asked to dance by a punky, pink-haired woman with so many nose rings she looked like a bull. The wheelchaired woman clearly had salsa in her blood, and got up and danced like the best of them, her body still limber, not missing a beat, smiling. I noticed that some of the women had skins of very dark leather, deeply lined; they could pass as luggage. They wore the highest of heels, low-cut gypsy dresses with slits up to their earlobes. At first I thought, 'How could they come out looking like that?' but after I had watched them dancing they transformed before my eyes into seriously sexy-looking babes – even the women who looked like men. At one point, everyone formed a large circle, and one wizened but lithe older man shouted instructions. At lightning speed, every-one in the circle switched partners, not a step out of place, each person looping their arms over other people's heads with complicated precision and somehow without choking each other to death. I knew I was standing there on the side lines grinning like a proud mother, even though I didn't know anyone there. I loved them all. I started watching at five in the afternoon, then went to dinner. When I came back at eleven at night they were still going, no one out of breath, everyone still hoofing it – including the woman once in, now out of the wheelchair.

This, I thought, is the human race at its finest; these people weren't trying to be the best at anything, they didn't care what they looked like: they were free. I didn't for one second feel that I was alone, because the atmosphere made me feel that we were all part of this wonderful thing. These people were residents of the present, and I was catching it. I could learn so much from them, and not just salsa. I wondered why I go on about there being so much wrong in the world when so much is right. I started thinking that we all have it in us to be connected to each other in this way. All we need to do is somehow become less affected by the torrential incoming of unnecessary information and the pressure on us to be someone else. We don't have to do something in politics or start a new religion; we just need to learn to navigate the world we created so we can feel less isolated and frightened. This is who we are when we're not trapped by mayhem. We all have this potential to let it rip and feel this kind of joy. Even if it lasts only a little while, it will still affect us for the rest of our lives.

In the following chapter, I'll give specific mindfulness exercises for baby, child and parents. The adult and the older folks have to learn it without Mommy there to hold their hands, but they can use the six-week mindfulness course as a handbook. Our brains go through different growth stages at each phase in our lives. I believe we need bespoke exercises which are suitable for each. The solution is not a one size fits all.

7

Mindfulness for Parents, Babies and Children

Just one thing I'd like to point out here: when I talk about children and babies in this chapter, I am going to alternate between 'he' and 'she' so that I don't get run out of town for being sexist.

If you have just read the last chapter and you're a parent, you might be thinking, 'How do I use this mindfulness stuff? I don't even have time to do my own exercises, let alone take a shower, how can I do this with my kids?' Here's an example of a day you'll never have, but read it anyway – it might make you laugh.

A Day in the Life of a Parent and Their Child

7.30 a.m. You go into your child's bedroom to wake her up. Be gentle, and be early, so it's not all panic stations. (My mother used to scream my name because I was late every morning; she was like an air-raid siren announcing World War Three.) Remember to keep your tone soft and soothing.

8 a.m. At breakfast, ask your child to describe how her toast/ eggs/ cereal taste. How does the sensation of chewing feel? What's does the food feel like in her

mouth? Ask her if she'd like to choose to do one activity each morning and not think so much about it but sense what she's doing, for example, washing her hands/ putting on her shoes/ petting the dog . . . Each day she can pick something else, so it's always new.

8.30 a.m. Driving your child to school, you could play I Spy with My Little Eye, but do it with sound, so it becomes I Hear with My Little Ear and ask her to guess what sound you're listening to. This plugs her right into the experience of paying attention. You could also play this with smell. We rarely use this sense, but as long as your child is focusing on the subtleties of a sense, she's exercising her mind.

9 a.m. Your child starts her school day. Hopefully, some mindfulness training is part of the curriculum. (*See* the section on mindfulness in schools in Chapter 8.)

4 p.m. Plan another game for your child to play each day after school – say you're going to give her a fun quiz to do. One day ask her to count how many clouds she can see during lunch break. On another, ask her to notice how many people in the school hall are wearing something purple. How many teachers smiled that day? Each day, give her something to notice and ask her to tell you after school. Be curious and ask her for more details.

7 p.m. When you're eating dinner, make it a habit to chat about anything she feels like talking about. Don't have an agenda, just let it be a casual conversation. Stay curious and be interested, but do not pry. If you're anxious or exhausted, tell her, so that she won't think it's a reaction to her and that she sees that you have

emotions, too. (You, too, can throw a hissy fit.) Allow her to be in whatever mood she's in. She doesn't have to tell you why, but try to get her to talk about what she feels like inside.

8 p.m. At bedtime, read to her, but if there are any illustrations of the characters ask her if she can guess what they're really thinking about. It's only a guess; it's to get her used to looking below the surface, using her radar. You can also do this while watching TV by turning the sound down – but only for a few minutes or so, or she'll end up hating you.

Parenting without Tears

Every parent, at some time in their child's life, asks the question: 'Is it my fault?' No one really knows to what extent children develop as a result of nature and to what extent it's nurture: it has been a hot topic since the 1960s. They now say it's about 50/50 . . . so you only have a 50 per cent chance to screw up your child. The genes are the deck of cards he's been dealt, but how you play them is up to you.

The nature bit – the DNA – sets the blueprint with genetically pre-programmed brain cells, but they're awaiting your input, Mrs or Mr Nurture. The way you hold, smile, frown, sing, and say, 'Boo!' directly affects the circuits in your child's brain. And it is these which, ultimately, lay down his character, along with the culture, the environment and the people he meets in his life.

Read this now!

What follows are a couple of the most important rules for being a parent.

Know Thyself

I'm sorry to harp on but, if you want to be the best parent, your first mission is to 'know thyself'. The oracle of Delphi said this, and she didn't even have kids. This doesn't mean you have to dig down into the coalmine of your unconscious, but when you notice you're having a heated reaction to something that's going on and berate yourself for it, believe me, your kid will pick it up. As a matter of fact, when a baby feels that his mother is angry, depressed or anxious, he will absorb those feelings into himself rather than see his mother as flawed. If you're kind to yourself and not judgemental, your baby will also sponge up that compassion, making him feel safe and secure later in life.

All your past experiences will affect your kid *unless* you become conscious of your own issues. The danger lies in projecting our problems on to our kids, blaming them for our shortcomings as if they're a photocopy of us and as if, through them, we can make things right (*see* mothers who hothouse their twelve-week-olds to get them into Oxford).

How we interact with our children is influenced by the experiences we had with our own parents. In the same way that you're imprinting on your baby's brain, your parents did on yours. 'They fuck you up, your mum and dad,' as Philip Larkin so lovingly said. If you think your child acts out, look in the mirror.

The mind of a child is like new-fallen snow, and we come along stamping our gigantic galoshes all over it, leaving our imprints. Your parents dumped their stuff on to you, their parents dumped theirs on them, and so on back to the first vertebrate. If you want to stop this ancestral relay race of 'pass the flaws', all you need to do is to become conscious of those imperfections.

On the other hand, if you come equipped with a healthy dose of compassion, good genes and some knowledge about how your mind works, your child will be fine. And if you can stay present even when he's screaming his lungs out, you've won first prize in the Parenting Gold Cup.

It's interesting, though, to realize that, when your child is having a tantrum, the fury you initially associate with your child's upsetting behaviour may actually be coming from you. You might be reminded of some pain from your own childhood; the idea is to notice that the anger you sometimes feel towards your child might be fuelled by your own unresolved hurts.

Don't go into a full panic when you read this – most of us don't get it right all the time, if we're honest, but there are ways to make repairs, and it's never too late. If you find looking back to your childhood all too painful an experience, it might be an idea to consider some counselling.

I had no idea how to be a mommy. I didn't go to university to study how to wipe a behind or burp another human being.

But when they hand the baby to you, you feel this love *whoosh* through you. It's either pure love, or the morphine – which is why I had three children: I couldn't get off it. I had my children in NHS hospitals (thank you), and ended up sharing a room with a woman who had 'read the books'. I kept her up all night with questions like 'Why is it leaking? How do you feed it? Can I use your breasts for milking purposes?' The next day I was wheeled out and put in my own room. I told them that, just because I was on TV, I wasn't demanding special attention and I didn't mind sharing. The nurse told me that the woman had asked for me to be moved; she couldn't stand it. From then on, I depended on the kindness of nurses.

Your Baby is Not an Extension of You

God must have put an irresistible smell on the baby's head to stop you from flushing it down the toilet at the first tantrum, but after it fades, what keeps you interested in the baby is, I think, your belief that it's a reflection of yourself. Narcissus staring into the water and falling in love with his own reflection is how you gaze into the crib.

Then, suddenly, you realize this child is not you, he has his own quirks and mannerisms, and the baby that once adored you now has the audacity to break rank and march off to the sound of his own bugle call. Now, you can either celebrate that you've given birth to an individual and go, 'Hooray!' or you can attempt to take a mallet and beat that clay until it looks like you.

As a matter of fact, one of the first reactions after the baby's grand entrance is for the mother to imagine that he looks exactly like his father and a little like her. (In reality, he doesn't look like either of you – all babies look like smashed, bald prunes – but it's in our biology to imagine they resemble Daddy, to ensure that Daddy sticks around.) Also, if you think there's a sign that Baby's going to be a mathematical genius or a future tennis star, that is also down to your imagination. Early on, you should try to see your baby for what he is, not what you project on to him. Nature, in the name of survival, is using everything she's got to make you see this blue or pink package as containing all your dreams and hopes, otherwise you'd dump it. This 'thing' is the next 'you', and it will carry your genes into the future, so it's in your interest to believe the baby is going to be the next messiah.

I remember, I had an operation on my feet when I was a kid and I begged my mother to turn on the air conditioner; it

was boiling in Chicago – even the bugs melted. She wouldn't do it because she said it was a waste of money; the air would just escape. I begged her again; I couldn't get up, my feet were in bandages. She eventually went to the wall and pushed her finger, nowhere near the air conditioner, and went, 'Mmmmmmm,' imitating the sound it would make if it was on . . . like I wouldn't be able to tell the difference.

I'm in a constant state of vigilance, guns cocked, to make sure my mother's voice isn't coming out of me now.

She loved me as a generic baby but not specifically as me. She thought I would be a duplicate of her; she was very beautiful, while I had the teeth of a beaver. I was punished a lot because she couldn't understand that I had a different personality from her. We didn't know it then, but she had extreme OCD. She used to make my bed when I was still in it, hold a napkin under my chin when I ate fruit, sort my underpants in the order of the year I got them and chase dustballs on her hands and knees with sponges tied to every limb.

It simply was not acceptable for me to have any traits, habits or thoughts that were not hers. Maybe they should have given her a glove puppet rather than a child – it would have saved so much confusion.

It's crucial to try to see and love your child as he really is and to respect his tastes and proclivities (unless they involve collecting stuffed puffins). He doesn't need your criticism; he will get enough as he grows older. If you are practising mindfulness, you'll be able to feel what he feels and this empathy will bubble wrap him from the slings and arrows of future jerks.

My parents didn't really approve of me. They were in love with me when I was a cute, bouncing baby, but the minute I opened my mouth and words came out, the love affair was over. I have hunted most of my life to find people who like me the way I am.

In contrast to mine, Ed's parents were the stuff fairy tales are made of; maybe I married him partly for his parents. Nothing – but nothing – was too much trouble for them. Scones came out of Ed's mother day and night. She'd run up and fluff your pillow before your head hit it, and would practically be waiting there with a cup of tea when you woke up. Can you imagine me marrying into that? It reminded me of those Dickens stories where the orphan, after years of abuse, finally walks into the warm hearth of a happy home.

I used to choose my best friends in school based on who their mothers were. I usually went for the warm and over-weight Jewish mothers (not the crazy ones) who lived to cook and feed their offspring. I would sort of move in, hoping they wouldn't notice, like those stray kittens who, when they suddenly just show up during milking time, get included in the litter, and no one goes, 'Who the hell is that?' Likewise, the mothers didn't mind me being there; they were that loving, and knew something wasn't right in my own home. They never mentioned the fact that I lived in their refrigerator, gazing at all the fresh and homemade food. In our fridge, we had cigars and some coleslaw left over from when Kennedy was shot. I loved it when these mothers hugged me, being smothered in those large boobs and the smell of cinnamon cookies.

Parenting Mindfully

Noticing

If you're with your child and you're either reacting to his mood or, for some reason, you find your mind is going down the pan, *notice* it (that alone will earn you seventy-five gold stars). When you're in the clutches of a negative takeover, do not at this point converse with your child, instead, even if you have to make an excuse, go and sit in another room and try to do a minute of mindfulness. (If that doesn't work, take Xanax or swig vodka.) When the feeling has diffused in your mind, return to your child, even though you still may want to run for the hills. Only when you're steady can you solve your own and therefore your child's problems.

Labelling

When you're with your child (or, really, whoever you're with) and beginning to feel yourself quivering with rage, anxiety or frustration, try to label the emotion you're experiencing, either in your mind or by writing down the one word that describes what you're feeling. This labelling process stops the rumination, when you build up a story about all the reasons you're furious, which results in a tidal wave of cortisol. Those feelings will be dampened down as you move your focus from the primitive to the higher, more thoughtful prefrontal cortex. This is a great way to deal with amygdala hijack: 'Name it, don't blame it.' (I think I made that one up.)

Scanning

When you're interacting with your child, try to switch on your internal spotlight to scan for any tension in your body; posture and body language give away your state of mind. Eighty-five per cent of what we express is through our body language, not through verbal communication.

Check if you're reacting in your reptilian mode. If you are, you can bet your boots he's going to respond in his: 'Angry monkey see. Angry monkey do.' You can't really blame the child – he's a child, impulsive and wildly emotional; you're the one who is responsible for developing his prefrontal cortex.

Reflecting

When your child is highly stressed, angry or sad, try expressing in words what you think he might be feeling. So, if he's screaming about the fact that you threw out the five-year-old sock that he still sleeps with, maybe reflect back to him, for example, 'I can see that you're upset. It must feel terrible . . . I loved my sock, too, from when I was six. I should have asked you first.' Try to put yourself in his shoes so you'll feel what it's like to be missing a sock or without a shoe.

Your child's character is shaped by your early interactions with him. He learns emotions by mirroring your facial expressions. He can only learn to smile, stick out his tongue, make a sad or an angry face, from copying yours. So, when he is getting hot under the collar, use your face to portray interest, kindness and openness. Experiment with it and see if he begins to reflect back curiosity and kindness and forgets about the anger. It's not unheard of that, by changing our expression, we alter not only our mood but also that of our baby. Sometimes we can 'fake it to make it'; as long as you're doing it consciously, it's still mindful.

A reflective parent does not focus solely on the external behaviour of their child but also focuses on him as an individual with his own mind. The phrase 'he has a mind of his own' is often used in a slightly derogatory way to describe a wilful and stubborn child. A reflective parent appreciates this and remains non-judgemental, appreciating how different their child's mind is from theirs.

The Five-minute Whine

If you notice you're going into a violent game of verbal volleyball with your child – 'It's your fault.' 'No, it isn't, it's your fault.' 'No, you messed me up.' 'No, you did.' – this is a good time to try the following exercise.

As you're the parent, now's the time to shut up. Tell your child he has one minute (set the timer on your phone) to give his side of the story without you interrupting (even if you're tearing every sinew in your body trying to restrain yourself from wringing his neck). As he rants, see if you can do the mindfulness of sound exercise, listening to his shouts as if they're just noise rather than getting caught up in the drama. Then focus in on what he's saying and see if he's changed in any way . . . Hopefully, he'll be calmer. The benefits of this exercise are that he's probably exhausted himself from his hissy fit, and you'll have brought down your cortisol levels.

Focusing

Just as you practised shining that spotlight of attention on a sense, in this exercise, take your focus to your child, paying attention to the details of what he's saying, so when he's telling you about how his rabbit was eaten by a fox you can feel the depth of the trauma and – here's the big challenge – put down your phone while you're listening.

My children sometimes ask me about when they were little. I can't remember – we have to watch videos to find out. When they were talking to me, I was only half listening.

If you do pay attention your cortisol level goes down, and when you become calm, your child becomes calm. If you're hyped up on adrenaline, he will fuel up on his. If you're oozing oxytocin, your child cooks up his own supply, and that particular hormone engenders the ultimate nurturing.

If you feel sudden hostility or negativity towards your child, even if he's mid-tantrum, do a short, visual mindfulness practice. Take your focus to a feature of his face, anchoring your attention as you would with sound or breathing. Focus on his face and investigate with curiosity that particular feature – the eyes, nose, or mouth – as if you've never noticed it before.

Backing Off

This is to wean you off that overwhelming urge to make it all better when your child is distressed. He needs to learn how to soothe himself; if you always do it, he'll have to find someone who looks like you to marry.

The idea of compassion shouldn't be confused with gushing sympathy, where you mollycoddle the kid, as in 'Oh, you poor baby, Mommy's here.' Like he can just feel better because you say so? Let him feel what he feels. Support him by reflecting back his feelings to show that you understand him and that his feelings can be dealt with. You're teaching him not to run away from his feelings but to turn towards them and learn that they're nothing to be afraid of, they're just feelings.

To sum it all up . . .

The responsibility of the parents changes depending on what age their child is, but the basic foundations remain the same: give unconditional love, lay down boundaries . . . and keep shovelling money out to them.

Babies

Each baby comes with a genetic blueprint and a range of possibilities which the body is programmed to develop; however, the program isn't automatic. It's switched on or off by external experiences. Think of the baby as an external foetus needing to be programmed by you or some nice other human nearby; otherwise, she'll just remain a sack of organs. The brain of a baby is shaped by her interactions with the world and her relationships. These stimulate neural firing and sculpt the connections. As your baby grows, there's a weaving together of genes and experiential input, and this is how a personality is born.

When you have a baby, you're so hyped up on love juice (you have to be, otherwise you'd never forgive her for destroying your body) that everything is euphoric: you're baking cupcakes with bows on them and suddenly find that pink is an acceptable colour. Then time goes by and, one sunny day, you find yourself in a state of wanting to kill. You have gone ballistic because of this person, only fifteen inches long, and bald, who can't even tell you what she needs, she just lies there screeching, and you're supposed to know what she wants – like you're Psychic Nell.

I used to go into high panic each time I was left alone with one of my kids when they were babies. I thought I wouldn't notice if they suddenly ate a plug or I left them in a shoe shop; I didn't trust myself with them. I spent most of my money hiring professionals; I even tried to drag a nurse home with me from the hospital. Gradually, I remembered that my mother didn't have a maternal bone in her body. She obviously didn't read the baby manual either, and used to leave me in my cot, shouting, 'Gargle, gargle, gargle!'; it's all I could come up with. Later, she read me stories from Grimm's Fairy Tales, where a bear always ate the children if they did something appalling like not finishing their soup. I now always finish not just my soup but everyone else's in the restaurant.

A Baby's Brain

Before I explain the following exercises, I'm going to give you a little tour of your baby's brain so that you can understand how and why she reacts to the world the way she does.

Even before she is cooked, while still in the float tank known as 'you' your baby is forming 25,000 neurons per minute. Every second, about 2 million synaptic connections are made. Each time those branches connect they're downloading traits and tendencies which have been perfected through all those previous generations. Imagine zillions of also-rans from the Beginning of Mankind – all those losers who didn't make the grade. Your baby is the survivor of the fittest of the fittest; first-prize winner in the evolutionary Grand Prix. There were probably humans in the past with webbed feet, but they became extinct, because ducks came along and could waddle better.

Right from when she was still in the womb, your baby can already assemble herself without a navigation system. Each cell innately knows which location it's meant to go to. An elbow cell knows to move to the elbow region (or Elbowville, as it's known), a toenail cell heads southward without a compass and finds the exact place it's meant to be. Can you imagine if there was a mix-up and your eyebrow found itself on your armpit? No amount of surgery could help. (Though if you ended up with a breast growing out of your forehead you could auction yourself off as a Picasso.)

Her body cells don't need your help to form a body; they know what they're doing and have been doing it for billions of years. To create the brain is where you – Mommy, Daddy or caregiver – need to step up to the challenge. You are now the master builder. Four weeks after conception, half a million neurons are being manufactured every minute, more than your baby will ever have again, so you have to take this opportunity with all the plentiful neural crops to connect the ones she'll need if she's going to flourish in a particular environment. You'll help her strengthen the neurons she'll need, and the ones she doesn't need will just wither away. It's called neurogenesis (a great name for a band).

For example, if your baby is born in the Western world, she probably won't need the skills for blowing out a nose dart or skinning a whale (unless she's from Canada), so the neurons that would establish those talents atrophy. This process of the weakest cells being culled is known as Neural Darwinism. In the same way, when your baby begins her life she has an almost limitless repertoire of sounds she can create, but only the words and sounds that she hears repeated will construct her own native language.

So if you make those clicking noises to her on a daily

basis, she will be able to speak Xhosa by the time she's twenty. In narrowing the sounds down, the other synapses that would have developed her knowledge of other languages don't connect, so she may learn another language later in life but she'll never get that accurate sound of phlegm being coughed up that you get with, say, a native German speaker.

Learning to Pay Attention

We learn to pay attention at the beginning of our lives, then we just forget it later on because we get too distracted by all the choices we have. Your baby's attention becomes riveted on an object until she finally comprehends its name, its colour, its shape, then she moves on to the next object. Your baby instinctively pays attention while relentlessly repeating, 'Wa' and pointing to a car. Luckily, Mommy doesn't (normally) jump down her throat, giving her, 'Shut up already, you got it all wrong.' She corrects her baby and squeals with delight when she finally gets a word right. With each correct word, the baby gets a hit of dopamine, so she's motivated to learn the next word. A baby, like an animal, has the ability to be completely present with her feelings, whether she's happy, sad, scared or angry. By the time you're an adult, you're usually covering up those feelings, feeling guilty for having them or neatly tucking them into your pants so they never show up in public again.

Exercise: Tuning into Baby

Bring your attention to where your body is in contact with whatever you're sitting, lying or lounging on, and switch your attention away from the chattering mind to the physical sensations you are experiencing. Now move your attention to your breathing, maybe counting from one to ten. Gently pick up your baby and hold her so her heart makes contact with yours. Imagine that when you breathe out your breath is going into her heart, and when she breathes out it's going into your heart. Notice if your heartbeats synchronize. Lastly, hold your baby away from you and look into her eyes, observing what's there, without projecting your emotions on to her, just being in the moment.

Now, start rocking gently. The normal Motherese that spills out of your mouth (remember the 'Whooogie, woo, woo, doo dee doo') is what calms and soothes your baby. So make those cooing sounds and watch her reactions . . . all babies love this one. Your tone is as important as your facial expression.

Tragically, I didn't have any of this information, so I had to develop my own methods. When my daughter Marina used to start screaming, for whatever reason, I used to join in like it was a competition for who could shout loudest, and that made her stop mid-shriek in surprise and then laugh. This may not work for all babies, so tread carefully. As she got older, she demanded I sing at top volume at her parties for entertainment. Her favourite tune was the theme of _The Flintstones_ sung in the style of Ethel Merman. It was so piercing that the ears of the other, traumatized children were bleeding.

The benefit of this exercise isn't just to create that Kodak moment or to have a fluffy experience – when a mother rocks her baby or holds her, she's unconsciously synchronizing their heartbeats, and when the baby sees her dilated pupils she instinctively senses that her parasympathetic system (calm) is aroused. This triggers a biochemical response of pleasure in the baby as her endorphins kick in. If the mother doesn't give good face, or holds her aggressively, or says sharply, 'No, don't do that!', it triggers a release of cortisol and her sympathetic system becomes active. I had a few too many 'no's from both my parents. That's why I'm usually ready for battle even in my sleep.

Mirror Neurons

The thing that really helps to attune mother and baby (though some scientists say this is bunkum) is what are known as mirror neurons. These particular types of neurons, found in various parts of the brain, seem to provide an explanation for how one state of mind can imitate that of someone else, by linking motor action to perception. Let me explain. The parent's emotions (shown by their facial expressions) will automatically fire similar neurons in the baby's brain and create identical expressions; if you smile, she smiles.

You can think of yourself as an emotional mirror that gives psycho-feedback any hour of the day and night. It's as if you asked me how I was and I had to stare into my girlfriend's face to give you an answer. This is probably why comedians become comedians – because they have a deep need to see thousands of faces smiling back in order to know they feel okay. If those faces aren't there or if they look bored, the comedian feels empty and abandoned. (I made that up; it may not be a fact.)

Anyway, if a parent smiles, the baby feels good; if they look mad, the baby feels bad. Our brains are directly wired to our facial muscles, so every spurt of chemicals and neural connectivity is directly linked to our faces by our nerves. If some warm and cosy oxytocin is cooking upstairs, our mouths may lift and our eyes twinkle, creating a smile. Basically, if your mother always looked at you with a scowling face, you're pretty much screwed.

A Pot-pourri of Facial Expressions and Their Effects

Smiling Face Every face you pull influences the way your baby perceives herself. That's not to say that the parent should smile approval all the time (this would probably plant the seeds of narcissism) and make the baby believe that she's the greatest being on earth when, actually, she's a putz (Jewish expression for loser).

Faking the Face If your baby believes that Mommy or Daddy is faking it, she'll suspect that people she meets later in her life are phoney. She also is being taught a lesson in how to cover up her feelings (which is only useful if she is going to be a stewardess).

Angry Face If a parent has a cross face when a child is distressed, chances are she'll have a touch of anxiety later on – or have a tic like Mr Bean's.

Disapproving Face Each time the baby gets this look, she experiences a feeling of alarm that is accompanied both by a high level of cortisol and a dose of shame.

Dead Face This is the most debilitating of all expressions: the no expression face. Even an angry face would be better, because at least then your baby is getting a reaction. With the dead face she doesn't feel she even exists, so she doesn't develop a sense of self.

Nice Face If Mommy soothes her baby by showing her looks of love, understanding and compassion, the chances are greater that she's building a well, better-balanced baby.

By the way, there are fifty different kinds of smiles (smug, sneering, gloating, patronizing): make sure you're using the right one. Get the smile right, or your child will be sneering at you for ever.

Mindfulness for Children

The saying for child-rearing that really helps me is 'Connection rather than correction'; it prompts you to re-establish a connection with your child when you've had a bit of a rocky encounter. What do you think? Is it as hard for you to be reflective all the time?

Your baby will miraculously become a child at around the age of four. At this point he'll ask you questions like 'Does peanut butter come from heaven?' 'Does a baby come out when you blow your nose?' I'm not an expert at answering these questions, so I just said 'yes' to everything . . . that's why they still wait for Santa, aged twenty-six.

It's never too early to understand the brain, so my first suggestion is to show your child a drawing of what it looks like and to explain how it works. Help him understand that everyone has a similar set of reactions; everyone has an amygdala that registers danger, and that's why he'll have an urge either to beat up the bully or to scram. If he understands that we all share this equipment, he won't feel shame or blame. So when he's about to blow, hopefully, he'll be able to say, 'That's my amygdala firing – thar she blows!' If he understands the impact of high emotions or stress, he won't blame himself for losing his cool or not doing well in exams even after he's studied hard, because he'll know that one of the first things to go down when he's under too much stress is his memory.

This will also help him to understand when he's operating from his limbic brain, and this knowledge will automatically shift him into his prefrontal cortex, his Captain America brain. You can also use Barbies and/ or Transformers as visual aids to demonstrate the different functions of each brain. But the perfect aid for illustrating the shift from limbic to prefrontal has to be the Incredible Hulk.

It may seem as though your child craves independence, but at this point he still needs to know you're close by – you're still God-like until he becomes a teenager, and then you're loathsome. You, as God for now, are the source of all safety and security. So the most important thing to remember (as I've said before) is not to dump the luggage from your past on to him.

Your child's brain is still under construction, and one of your jobs is to help him understand why he does what he does, even if you have no idea. Stepping into someone else's shoes is called mentalization, a term coined by clinical psychologist and psychoanalyst Peter Fonagy and his colleagues. It's the capacity to understand your own and therefore other people's behaviour, motivations and intentions. Mentalization is a particularly effective skill for parents to have, because the child doesn't know how to make sense of what he's feeling. With your help, eventually, he will. If you bark at him, he'll bark back. If you're caring and genuinely curious, without your own agenda lurking in the wings, you'll be able to influence his biology positively. Remember: experience shapes brain structure, and how you treat your child will shape who he is and who he'll become.

When your child does something that you find unacceptable (as in try to push his sister down the stairs) try to notice your reaction. If it's tyrannical and you let it loose, you'll never get him to tell you his side of the story honestly. He'll just go into defence mode. See if you can be stern and yet compassionate . . . and if you can do that, you'll be canonized.

I once fell in love with a lizard when I was a kid on holiday in Jamaica with my parents. I named him Alvin and spent days gleefully watching him leap from ceiling to wall to floor. My mother tried to flush him down the toilet, which broke me. No warning: straight down the pan. Obviously, I was traumatized, otherwise I wouldn't still remember it.

It got worse. I got another lizard, called him Alvin 2 and, unbeknownst to my mother, packed him in my suitcase to take him home to Chicago. I thought he would be able to breathe between the clothes. At Customs, they opened our bags and there he was, spread-eagled and stiff. My mother gave me hell, not recognizing the depth of my love for Alvin.

Peter Fonagy writes that parents who can read their child's mind while understanding what's going on in their own minds have something called 'reflective functioning', which promotes good social skills and the ability to manage and regulate their own emotions. A reflective parent sees their child as having a mind of his own, which (for some reason) is often used in a slightly derogatory way to describe a bolshie child. So when Fonagy uses the term 'reflective parenting', he means the style of child-rearing that we all dream of. To be able to listen patiently and enter the mind of the monster that is squishing toast into your hairdryer is, of course, beyond most of us.

Exercise: Be Inquisitive, Not an Inquisitor

If you, as a parent, find yourself facing a lizard-type situation (*see* Alvin), first, maybe do a little mindfulness and, when you feel settled, ask your child, calmly, to tell you what exactly he loves about the lizard. This doesn't mean that, afterwards, you should say, 'Get a hundred lizards if it makes you happy,' but, before you start laying down the law, at least acknowledge your child's point of view. Don't just throw in, 'Okay, so the lizard died. We all die. Don't be such a cry-baby, you're a big boy now.' Instead, say something like 'Maybe he'd be happier outside jumping from plant to plant with his friends rather than smashed up in a suitcase. What do you think?' He may just go along with this. If you're curious about your child's feelings, it releases feel-good endorphins in him so, when you explain your point of view, he's not so defensive.

Here are a few things to think about.

- What were your internal thoughts and feelings when the situation arose?
- If you had a trigger response of negativity, how did you manage to stabilize yourself?
- What were the child's reactions before and after the exercise?
- Do you like lizards any more now?

Dealing with Emotions

Don't try to make everything better when your child feels a hot emotion. Humans are built to feel the whole palette of emotions, so let him experience as many as he can, even though you're dying inside that he's hurting. Emotions aren't to be avoided, so don't bring out the cotton wool too soon;

he needs to build up some coping mechanisms so that, later in life, he's resilient when things don't go his way.

When Max was little we went to a party in the park and he was bullied on the bouncy castle. I was devastated that someone could do this to my perfect son and make him suffer. Max didn't even notice or seem to mind. But I went into full terrorist mode, got up on that bouncy castle and tried to choke the bully. Max was appalled. (It can't have been a pretty sight either, as I was also eight months pregnant so kept losing my balance and falling over.)

Sure, I made mistakes as a parent, but you couldn't say I wasn't upfront with my emotions. Some parents keep their feelings locked away and smile like loons even though they're furious inside. Their children will smell a rat but won't be able to untangle their confusion. So, when their child is grown up, he'll smile just like them, and just like you have all that rage juice simmering in his basement. If you express your emotions in a non-threatening way, your child will be able to deal with his own.

Exercise: Dealing with Emotions

When your child is in the grips of a negative emotion, sense the impact it has on your own emotions and, without trying to repress or deny them, focus in on the feelings in your body rather than the stories in your head (*see* mindful emotions in the six-week mindfulness course). The point of mindfulness isn't to try to feel good, it's about being able to relate to negative emotions as if they're just a physical phenomenon – they don't need to be analysed. When you feel your mind has cooled down from the red mist of panic, you'll be able to listen to your child without your trip-wire hot reaction and be able to reflect his feelings, maybe saying something like, 'That really must have hurt. I would have felt bad, too, if that happened to me.' The idea is to validate him instead of smothering him with, 'There, there. Mommy's here. Everything will be okay now.'

Story-telling

Being told stories is how children make sense of themselves and of the world. Only the names of the characters change; stories are archetypes and the themes are universal. The stories usually set up a moral compass with a bad guy and a good guy; the good guy usually wins, mainly because they're good (except in German fairy tales, where wolves devour whole families for reasons unknown, other than to Messrs Grimm, the authors). Usually, a fairy godmother type is thrown into the mix to spice things up and provide a great excuse for a costume change. Stories help to establish the child's own autobiography, to give some narrative to his life, and a strong sense of self.

We are the only species who tell stories; no other animal on earth can do it . . . ask them, and they'll give you nothing, probably just moo at you and walk away.

I assume you're already reading stories to your child. If not, why not? Anyhow, now take some time (but only if he's in the mood) to suggest that maybe one time, instead of listening to the story, he could tell his own personal story so far. Whatever he says, listen, and keep your attention focused on the story and on his demeanour. If he gets bored or doesn't want to continue, drop it. Usually, when you listen with energy, he'll be energized, and if you're curious and compassionate, he'll be excited and motivated to keep going.

Exercise: Puppet Time

Ask your child to tell you a story, any story. You'll learn a lot about him by his choice of plot, the characters and the way he tells it. If he doesn't want to, don't push it. Or maybe he would like to use a few dolls or action figures to help tell the story. Maybe one doll is your child, and another toy is you, Daddy or the caregiver. It may be revealing to discover how your child perceives your relationship not just with him but with the whole family. Whatever happens, don't interrupt or make suggestions: keep shtum.

Exercise: Early Self-regulation

Before I get to the actual exercise, I want to stress that one of the most important things any child has to learn is to be able to tolerate delay, to somehow hold back from instant gratification. To expect everything you want to happen right now will only lead to disappointment.

A famous experiment shows how the ability to hold back on instant satisfaction in childhood impacts on academic and social success later on in life. Four-year-olds were asked, each in turn, to sit in a room at a table with one marshmallow on it. The children were told that the experimenter was going to leave the room for five minutes and that they must not eat the marshmallow. If they refrained from eating it, they could have two marshmallows when the experimenter returned. Some of the children were also instructed that, when the person running the experiment left the room, in order to help them not eat the marshmallow, they should try not to think about what it would taste like but instead to pay close attention to its shape, colour and size. The ones who focused on these physical details did better at restraining themselves from eating the marshmallow than the ones who thought about the taste. This is a lesson in early mindfulness: focusing on an object in the moment means that you can't ruminate, whereas imagining the taste will cause endless frustrated thoughts of yearning to eat it and future thinking of how delicious it will be.

The children who showed that they could restrain themselves had a better-developed prefrontal cortex than the children who couldn't hold back. (Remember: a more developed PFC means more self-control, greater ability to pay attention and higher thinking.) The four-year-olds with the greatest self-control grew into teenagers who did better at school than their more impulsive peers. They had better attention and concentration skills throughout their lives.

You can't successfully train a child to resist a treat by badgering him. This causes stress, and he'll probably go for the whole bag and ram in every last one.

What you can do is to help him, using playful and innovative ideas, to learn how to hold back on his desires. You have to make it seem as if the child is taking control of his own emotions; you're only there in the background to catch him if things get rough.

Two great games for teaching young kids to make use of their developing prefrontal cortex are Simon Says and Musical Statues. Following instructions on cue is a magic key when it comes to self-control. The better your child is at stopping when the music stops or making the right movements on command during Simon Says, the stronger his prefrontal wiring for cognitive control becomes. The real first prize should go to the kid who can say 'no' to his impulses.

Exercise: Feeling Like a Snow Globe

Give your child a snow globe as a present. If, for some reason (like you've been in a coma since you were born), you don't know what this is, it's one of those clear balls which usually have some sentimental, or touristy, scene stuck to the bottom, maybe Jesus in his crib glued in there with the three kings. When you shake up the globe it goes into a frenzy of glitter or white snow. (Imagine how surprised Jesus would be if that had really happened.) When you hold the globe still, all the turmoil calms down. Suggest to your child that he might like to shake the ball and watch the turmoil turn to calm. Tell him he could use the snow globe when he feels unsettled or agitated, as a reflection of how he feels. The more angry or frustrated he feels, the harder he should shake it. When he holds it still, he should really focus on the spectacle happening in the ball. When the storm of glitter has settled, ask him if he can imagine that the flurry in the snow globe could be like the way he feels. Be casual and curious.

Here are some more things to think about.

- What was he feeling when he shook up the ball?
- What did he feel while he was watching the snow?
- Does he feel that his emotions have also calmed down, or not?

If he enjoys the experience and says it makes him feel calmer, tell him he can use the snow globe whenever he feels his emotions are taking him by storm. If he's about to take an exam, if a friend makes him angry or he feels the teacher's been unfair to him, he can just get out his secret snow globe, shake it and settle his mind along with the glitter. This will also train him to recognize when his mind is in high alarm and to realize that he can bring it back to the set point of calm without blaming his wobbly state on someone else. This is an example of early self-regulation. If your child learns this when he's young, by the time he's an adult he'll recognize when he's flipping into that limbic zone. Also, by keeping attention on his raw feelings without thinking about whose fault it is, he'll know that the feelings will eventually shift. They always do.

Someday, when he's about fifty-one, he may even be able to calm his mind without the snow globe but, if not, it's better than shooting heroin.

Exercise: Being an Owl

I based this exercise on one from a wonderful book by Eline Snel called *Sitting Still Like a Frog*, a children's book to teach mindfulness through imaginative games. The author gives various exercises and there's a DVD in the back of the book. I'm going to give you my version. I hope Eline forgives me.

Ask your child to describe what an owl does while it sits perched on a tree branch. Hopefully, he'll say, 'It sits still and only moves its head and its eyes. It looks very alert and in control.' Now ask him to imagine being an owl, sitting very still on a tree branch without moving or flying away, and just to notice everything that's going on around him. You can tell him that an owl is very wise and notices everything. Ask him to notice the owl's feathers lifting when it breathes in and lowering when it breathes out, and to move his eyes like an owl would. After a while, ask him to close his eyes and try to hear every sound around him and any sound coming from inside of him. He should listen hard to every rustle and even to what seems to be silent. Now ask him, with his eyes shut, if he can smell anything.

After a while, ask him if he notices that his breathing is slowing down. If it is, ask him if he notices that his thoughts are calming down like his breathing. If he says they aren't, that's fine, too, because he's learning to pay attention and to notice how his body feels inside.

Tell your child that he can imagine being an owl, sitting still and feeling his feathers move up and down whenever he feels restless, scared or pressurized. He might feel calmer and able to concentrate more when he needs to deal with tests, bullying, or when he gets hurt by someone. Remember to say that everyone feels these scary emotions, so he shouldn't pretend they're not there or get even more scared, but notice them and then imagine being that owl who focuses only on what's in front of its eyes.

Imagining being an owl is also helpful when your child wants to go to sleep but can't because his mind is racing with worries, plans, excitement or rethinking what he could/should have done in a certain situation. Tell him he can imagine what the owl would do when it goes to sleep. It would probably close its eyes and let all the thoughts come and go, and then just imagine its feathers moving up and down with each breath.

Then your child can say, 'Nightie night, owl.' You can then go to your bed and pretend to be an owl, too.

8

Mindfulness for Older
Kids and Teenagers

Mindfulness in Schools

William James, a renowned psychologist, wrote, 'The faculty to voluntarily bring back wandering attention, over and over again, is the very root of judgement, character and will. An education which improved this faculty would be an education par excellence.'

(And I would have said it if he hadn't.)

It should be compulsory that mindfulness is taught in schools. It doesn't take a genius to figure out that if the students were developing social and emotional skills besides reading, writing and . . . whatever that last one is (I didn't flourish in school), then there might be a drop in crime, in self-harming, drug abuse, and in the rates of mental illness and even suicide. I hope someone in the government is reading this.

On a smaller scale, if this latest generation could possibly learn to be less greedy than we were, they just might be able to save the planet we've trashed. What I mean by emotional intelligence is learning how to relate to other earthlings, creating trust and rapport and – dare I say it? – compassion. We aren't really specializing in those skill sets now, and it turns out that some of the brightest end up as the most emotionally stunted. They have brains, but these high achievers are sometimes the ones who screw the rest of us folk the hardest and have no conscience about it either (*see* Bernie Madoff, the board of Enron, Martha Stewart, etc.).

These days, kids are force-fed information in order to get the grades. Who cares if they really understand the subject as long as they memorize the facts and ace the exams? When we're pumped too full of pressure, the first thing to crash and burn is memory. How do we expect kids to flourish or learn anything when they're pushed to extremes to get high grades and then they can't remember anything? Kids' brains are like little landmines that can go off later in life if they're put under too much pressure.

I used to be interested in history – until I had to cram the entire Mesopotamian Empire into my brain in one night . . . and then got a D. I never spoke about it again. Mesopotamia was out of the picture for the rest of my life. Shame. There were so many subjects I'd have been interested in studying, but I knew, with all of them, that the day would come when I'd have to spew my knowledge on to a piece of paper in a limited amount of time. So I lost my erection for education quite early on.

Forget being inspired by anything: your mission, as a child, is only to get into the next school, and the next, and the next; there will always be something you have to get into next. I could never distil all the information I was given on a course into a well-crafted essay; I write how I talk, and sometimes there is no end to a sentence. This is why, now, I don't know any history, maths, languages or most of the other subjects I flunked with flying colours.

If you don't fail, you don't fight. It's the innovators who try, fail, try, fail . . . those are the real winners. It should be written on every epitaph: 'S/he tried.' Every new invention and creation was originally met with derision. There are many people who tend to fight original ideas, mainly because they don't have them. Teachers should teach kids to go for the great idea with no fear of getting an F on spelling when they're writing up their opus. Mozart probably couldn't spell and neither could any Mesopotamian. (I learnt that much.) Rather than teachers being made to concentrate on ramming information into the kids' minds so they can regurgitate it on the test paper later and forget it the next day, they should be in the business of igniting their little imaginations. You don't fatten a pig by weighing it.

While I'm on my roll, I think schools should also teach a course on the art of failing. Students need to know how to deal with failing as early as possible because, later in their lives, they're going to be carpet-bombed with it. If they seriously believe that their status as Captain of the Team is going to continue after they graduate from school, they'll find themselves badly shot down in flames with third-degree burns.

This is why the most popular cheerleaders often end up as crack whores. They weren't ready for the big, wide world; they didn't learn the lesson of all lessons: you cannot be perky for ever. A set of smiley choppers, big bazookas and pigtails just don't cut it when you're forty-five.

Excerpt from a Speech I Made at My Kid's Graduation from Secondary School

I was asked to give the keynote address. The year before, it was Daniel Craig . . . what a dip. I decided to make it a celebration of failure. So here it is.

I did not flourish at school. I began as a D student but I was sometimes a C student with criminal tendencies – they wrote my mother that. My typing teacher also wrote, 'Ruby has the mind of someone who will end up in jail.' My speciality subjects were pranks and smoking in the ladies' loo. I also provided ear piercing in the stalls.

I would do anything to avoid having to go to school, so I put raw fish in the lighting fixtures on the ceiling; the whole school had to be evacuated and no one ever found out where the smell was coming from or who did it. I made a volcano in science class that set the school on fire. I couldn't concentrate because of a rocky home life so I was put in the remedial English class where no one spoke a first language or a last language. We were asked to read our favourite poem, but no one knew one, so some of us just read the lyrics of popular songs; anything else was too taxing. I also remember getting such low SAT scores that my mother insisted something had be wrong with the grading machine and made me take them again. When they asked on the test which one of these doesn't fit with the rest – a rhinoceros; a dog; an eagle; an artichoke – I could not give an answer. I saw no difference.

I think the reason I failed at so much was because everyone gave up on me. It's true I was weird, but the point of going to school is to ignite something to give you a lust for curiosity. If you can keep that curiosity alight, the rest of your life will be the equivalent of getting an A star, without having to be a star.

Curiosity makes us superior to the animals. Sadly, many people don't use it. They have it, but it has become obsolete from non-use. Most people I meet don't ask questions, and these include some of the most brilliant people, with IQs off the planet. To me, they have no curiosity and are therefore idiots. We are born with this feature, so when is it taken away? As children, we hunger for information, we're insatiable; we don't even care what the story is, we just want to be stimulated. Then comes school. What kills the spark of curiosity is the fact that everything hangs on a grade. Nothing will burn out an interest more quickly. I'm aware that high grades might get you into a great university, where you will go to the best parties, but you can get hooked on this chasing-the-grade thing, and (even worse) if your parents push you too hard you might find that you get the habit of chasing a rabbit for the rest of your life, thinking that there's some reward in front of you, but it is always just out of reach. And when you conquer something, it might not be for the personal satisfaction of attaining a goal but instead be all about beating the competition. If you do it all for money or to impress others, including your parents, that way lies madness. Only if you find something you love is life worth living.

I know the teachers here have ignited a spark in a subject for each one of you. Somebody must have ignited something in me, because when the first act of my life ended (I couldn't do television any more) I needed to start over. Personally, this broke me for a few years, but I remembered that I had loved psychology once so I jumped on the last plane out of Depressionville and went back to school a few years ago to study it. This time, there was no one to nag me to fight for a grade. And if I managed to perform that quantum leap, anyone can do it. Just learn how to fail well and then get up again . . . and if you don't fit in the box, that's great, you'll invent a new box.

I'll just end with this saying, because I love it: 'This life is a test. Only a test. Had it been an actual life, you would have received further instructions on where to go and what to do.' Live every minute true to yourself.

Mindfulness is, at last, being taught in schools. Goldie Hawn's MindUP programme has been very successful in the US, and is now being used over here, too. One of the most successful mindfulness-in-schools programmes in the UK is called .b (dot bee). This project was devised by Chris Cullen and Richard Burnett, among others. In order to teach .b the teachers must go through an eight-week mindfulness training course themselves, because they need to be able to walk the talk. The programme is designed for secondary-school kids (between eleven and eighteen years old), and there's also a programme for primary-school kids (between five and eleven) called Paws b., which uses animation, film clips, games, etc. Exercises can be downloaded from http://mindfulnessinschools.org/what-is-b/sound-files/.

Teaching Your Older Kids Mindfulness

Here are a few of my favourite exercises from .b, which parents can try at home on their kids – unless they happen to be in full battling mode. Then skip it.

The Wild-puppy Brain

.b uses the image of comparing an untrained puppy to a child's untamed mind. First they talk about what the puppy does: makes a mess, yelps, tries to jump on you, bites your toes and is generally far too frisky. The other thing puppies do is try to be helpful by bringing you things, like an old chewed-up doll's head. This is a good image to show how our minds work: we want to think about something specific but our mind keeps bringing us all this irrelevant stuff.

The kids are asked, 'What would happen if you scolded the puppy to make it behave?' (They might say it would run away and hide.) 'What would happen if they ignored the puppy?' (It would keep yelping and jumping up.) If you told the puppy to pay attention, he wouldn't know what you were talking about, because he only speaks Bark. In the .b course they say that the mind is like a puppy, only it creates bigger messes.

By now you will have got the hang of this and realize that this metaphor is used to teach the kids that everyone's mind behaves like a puppy unless we treat it calmly and kindly, rather than getting furious with ourselves for having such a jumpy mind (which just makes us jumpier).

Exercise: Pay Attention

To practise using that skill of intentionally paying attention, ask your child/children to sit cross-legged on the floor with their spines up straight but not held stiffly. Then tell them to send focus to their toes (maybe even to each toe at a time). They can zoom into each body part and investigate the sensations. Is it tingling? Fizzing? Pulsing? Numb? This sharpens your child's ability to notice the difference between thinking about a part of their body and experiencing the sense of it. Make sure they know that, if they don't feel anything, that's okay, too, because at least they noticed.

The kids are told to send their attention (like shining a narrow beam of light) to each of these areas in turn:

Hands (maybe each finger)

Feet (maybe each toe)

The right knee

The left elbow

The right earlobe

The left eye

. . . And now the nose, feeling the breath going in and out through the nostrils. (Is the breath cool, warm, long, short?)

At the end ask your child to imagine opening up the lens of the torch to take in her whole body, breathing. She should imagine that her body is like a balloon that expands and deflates, expands . . . and so on.

Then she should open her eyes and stretch her whole body.

Exercise: Two-minute Challenge

Ask your child to focus on her breathing wherever she feels it most in her body: in her nose, stomach, chest . . . If this is too hard, she can count her breath up to ten, and then start over again if she wants to. If she's counting her breath, she should go, 'In-breath/ out-breath is one. In/ out is two . . .' and so on.

The idea is to see if she can keep her focus on her breath in that spot for two minutes. When the mind wanders, tell her to be nice, like she would be when disciplining the puppy, and then take the focus back. This is called aiming and sustaining.

Monkey Mind

Another lesson focuses on learning to stay calm when the mind gets too stormy.

Tell your child that her mind has a wild life of its own. Like a monkey jumping frantically from one branch to another, the mind jumps from idea to idea. If your child starts to get frustrated or is mean to the monkey, she might notice that it only gets more frenetic.

Exercise: FOFBOC

Introduce your child to FOFBOC, which stands for 'feet on the floor; bum on the chair'.

FOFBOC is a first-aid helper, when your child notices that her 'monkey mind' has taken her over and is dragging her from tree to tree. She can then use it as an anchor.

Tell her to sit on the floor or on a chair and send her attention to her feet where they make contact with the floor; she should also sense what her socks, shoes, toes, heels and soles feel like. Then she should focus on the sensation of where her bum is touching the floor or the chair. Ask her to imagine opening up the lens of her torch (her mind's eye) to take in the whole body.

Exercise: Breathing

Another tool your child can use when she's in her 'monkey mind' is simply to pay attention to her breathing (taking long in-breaths and long out-breaths), not to try to make her thoughts slow down or disappear, but just to watch them. After a while, she might notice that her mind/ the monkeys slow down and get tired. She also might start to notice that thoughts just swing around of their own accord and you don't have to take them so seriously: they're just thoughts acting like crazy monkeys, doing their thing.

Rumination

Tell your child about this endless daisy chain of thinking known as rumination (and that we all do it). It's where we think things like, 'Why didn't I get invited to the party? It's because no one likes me. I don't even like me. Why don't I like me? Because everyone thinks I'm creepy. Why am I so creepy? Because I'm creepy and they don't like me. Why don't they like me? Because . . .' This is the kind of stuff that keeps you up all night.

The word 'rumination' comes from what cows do when they digest grass: they chew it again and again before they swallow it, and it doesn't end there: they then bring it back up . . . and chew it again. That's what we do: a lifetime of chewing.

Exercise: Beditation

'Beditation' is to be used at night when your child can't get to sleep.

Encourage her, instead of trying to figure out why she's so creepy and why no one likes her, to do another version of FOFBOC – a lying-down body scan.

You could join in with this one. Both of you, lie on your backs, arms at your sides. First pay attention to your breathing and where exactly you feel it in your body. Take long, slow, deep breaths, and on each out-breath feel your body ground into the bed on the floor. Allow all the tension to drain away. You should feel the full length of your body, and focus your attention into your arms, your legs, the trunk of the body, your shoulders, neck and head. If you notice any tension in any area, start to imagine breathing into it, and then out again. The in-breath helps you focus into the area of tension and the out-breath helps you to imagine letting it go. Also, when you feel tension, send your focus as far away from your head as possible, to your feet, feeling them as if from the inside. Feel the breath filling your body getting heavier with each inhalation and each exhalation. With any luck, this should end in dreamland.

Exercise: Being Here and Now

This exercise is about the child finding the present and learning the skill of being able to go and visit it when she wants to. Ask your child to notice when she's on autopilot. Does she notice where her mind is while she is brushing her teeth, taking a bath or playing a game? Tell her that we all need to be on autopilot sometimes, but not all the time. The direct way of getting to the present is to plug into one of her senses: listening to a certain sound, tasting a chocolate, smelling a flower, touching a frog, whatever . . .

Exercise: Eating Mindfully

Have your child eat a chocolate as she usually would, and ask if she actually tasted it. Does she want to put another one into her mouth before she's even swallowed the one she's eating? This is being on automatic pilot.

Now tell your child to take a piece of chocolate, or a bite-sized piece of whatever treat she loves, and examine it as if she's never seen anything like it before: the colour, the contours, the shape. Now tell her to bring it up to her nose and smell it. Deliberately slowing down each action, she should put it on her tongue and then between her teeth, then chew on it, experiencing and savouring the details of the taste while chewing. Welcome to the present moment.

Life isn't always going to be a bowl of chocolates – there are going to be things in life your child won't like – but she needs to be aware of those moments, too.

Tell your child to go and get some sort of food that she doesn't like. It could be an olive – I hated them at that age, then got old and now love them. Ask her to do exactly what she did with the chocolate. She may not like the taste, but she should go through each step noticing with curiosity what the feeling is of disliking something, noticing how hard her mind is telling her to stop and spit it out. This teaches her that, even if things aren't great, still to be open to the experience.

Exercise: Thoughts aren't Facts

Ask your child to do an exercise called 'cloud spotting', where she sees thoughts as clouds passing by. Have her look up and notice how the clouds come and go, no matter if some are heavy or light, or stormy or bright. They all come and go.

Ask her to think of the thoughts in her mind as a radio, and to listen to the thoughts with detachment, letting them play in the background but not paying much attention to them.

This is helpful when thoughts (like tunes) come into her head like 'I'm stupid. I'm not good enough. No one likes me. [And the old favourite] I'm creepy': she can let them play but not take them personally – they're just tunes, not the truth. They can't hurt if she doesn't give them power or take them seriously.

Exercise: Learning to Deal with Bad Things

Feelings, like the thoughts, will come and go. You can't avoid bad things happening, but your mind can make it worse.

On an outline drawing of a body, ask your child to draw where she feels stress in her body. She can make a list of things that stress her out, for example, exams, feeling left out, feeling creepy, and then a list of how these impact on her body: headaches, sweating, heart palpitations, stomach ache. Now, if she can learn to focus only on the physical sensations and not on the thoughts, she'll notice that feelings come and go: they aren't facts, they're just feelings. Whatever happens, she shouldn't ignore or try to repress these feelings; they're always there, so the only way to deal with them is to stare them straight in the face or, in this case, focus on the feelings, and accept them. Don't feed them.

Okay, School's Out.
This is All about Gaming Mindfully

Kids aren't going to stop gaming and, if you try to curb them, good luck. We can discuss how good or bad games are for their minds, but they're here, and there are more coming. Some teenagers will refuse to learn mindfulness not only from school but from anyone. I'm starting to think that, maybe, a way to teach them mindfulness is through gaming, sharpening their ability to focus on specific goals while resisting distractions.

My son Max is a designer and coder and is working on creating the technology for combining stress reduction and emotional intelligence in games. Being his mother, I'm mentioning him because that's what my mother did to me. I hated her for it.

A Photo a Day

Usually, Instagram revolves around finding out how popular someone is by how many 'like's they can hustle up. A few thumbs-down can really stoke up that sense of failure. The idea for this is to take a picture of a scene or a person that grabs your attention and pulls you into the present; not just a snatched selfie but a moment you really want to savour. When you stop to really take in what's in front of your eyes, the noisiness in your mind subsides, and that, my friends, is a moment of mindfulness. This is a great way to store up your memories because, probably unlike other times, you'll remember that you were there. You can start to share those mindful moments with friends so everyone catches on to the idea.

Another Max Idea: Cold Turkeying

Here's an idea of how to come off the addiction of snorting something digital all day. We feel relieved any time we get a *ping*, *bleep*, cricket sound, moose cry, the sound of a guillotine being dropped, or whatever your ringtone is because we feel someone somewhere is thinking of us – even if it's a wrong number. The problem is, shortly after the *ping* you're right back to where you started: feeling lonely and isolated. This is the state of affairs, so, to counteract it, when you need or want to pay attention to the task at hand, set your phone to approximately how long you want to stay focused. During that time, it shuts down, as does your computer, so you can't tweet, Facebook, email, take a photo, watch Netflix or use Grindr or Tinder. Now focus on your work and, when you notice the urge to plug into something (you can bet it will happen), sense where the urge is in your body and gently take your focus back to where it was. When the timer finally beeps it should be the sound of celebration: people applauding, a whole orchestra with a choir singing in your honour, or the Queen personally thanking you. See if you can set the timer a little bit longer each day. Then, at the end of the week, just like God, you should rest for a day. One of the best things about this activity is that you're actually using a phone in order to avoid its distraction. Another win-win.

I think that gaming in the future should be less about killing the bad guy and more about negotiating with him. Trying to get into his mind to feel what he feels and then making choices based on that. There are already games around that teach you to read other people's emotions, such as *Tell Tale's Walking Dead*, which is all about creating social bonds in a high-stakes environment. Some games around now are good for training serial killers; the next generation of games might teach emotional intelligence. We need to stop seeing each other as good or bad guys. We're all people with multiple identities, parts of us are angelic, other parts evil. We need to learn a little empathy because we're all pretty much the same, under our various hair-dos.

Teenagers, Read My Lips: 'It is Not His Fault'

We all go through it, every human being on this earth: puberty is going to happen and has been happening for thousands of generations. Pimples are universal and will sprout on a Zulu as well as a Swede. A planetary mood swing starts at the age of eleven for girls and lasts until eighteen, and for boys it starts at thirteen and finishes around twenty-four . . . and, for some, it never ends.

Raising a teenager makes the terrible twos seem like a holiday in Hawaii. But your child's erratic behaviour isn't something he's doing on purpose to torture you, it's because his brain is going through a transformation, so don't roll your eyes and declare to the world that your kid is a lazy sea-slug and a maniac (if you recall, you were once one, too, and your parents rolled their eyes). Your child doesn't know how to self-regulate at this point. He's nuts one minute and Mommy's baby the next; it's like living with a newborn lion: one moment he wants to claw your eyes out and the next moment to nuzzle. The fact that this happens to everyone should be a great relief to parents. Understand that your teenagers are just developing normally for their age and they won't necessarily (as my parents thought) become serial killers.

Raising a teenager is so much less stressful if you understand that what's happening neurologically in that head has nothing to do with you. During this time, there's a window of opportunity to clean up the mess you might have made during the critical period when your child was a baby. The teen has another critical period when his neural connections re-wire, getting rid of the useless ones and laying down new ones, so here's your chance to help him re-sculpt.

There are circuits in the brain during the teen years that are noticeably different from those in childhood. As I mentioned, when your child's a baby, billions of neurons are growing at top speed. Those forests of neurons are there waiting to be filled with billions of bits of information; his brain is working like a sponge, absorbing pretty much everything that comes into eye and earshot.

At puberty, there's another monumental growth spurt of neurons to reprogramme the brain, and it's accompanied by chemical and hormonal changes. These changes happen independently from environmental influences or your nagging, so there's nothing you can do to stop them. You can shout as much as you want; it won't stop the oceans of testosterone or oestrogen that are about to spring forth in your child. The hormones start brewing while they're still a foetus: females are doled out oestrogen, males testosterone. You don't need me to tell you the outcomes of these differences, you can read millions of books on why men and women aren't and never will be on the same page. Testosterone can cause impulsiveness, aggression and an obsession with boobs. Oestrogen creates that flip-flop of emotions where you can fall in and out of love in seconds. Both genders have those mood swings, which accounts for why your teenager can swing from being Kate Middleton to Genghis Khan in seconds.

Things got worse when I hit puberty. The moment it struck, I went into shock. It's like my organs were just sitting around chewing gum, shooting the breeze and suddenly, *bam*! A big oestrogen rush, and my hormones started bubbling like Vesuvius about to blow. The harder my parents tried to discipline me, the harder I rebelled. My very reason for living was to overthrow the old regime and burn down the establishment . . . and I never cut corners. I didn't just run away from home at sixteen, I hitch-hiked my way through Europe, on money I had made from selling pot, to join an agitprop theatre group called Living Theatre who mainly performed nude (except for gas masks), and screamed in the audience's faces about how they were killing children. (I never found Living Theatre, because they had been jailed in Barcelona for obscene behaviour.) Later on, I helped close down my university for political reasons I didn't understand and now can't remember. We boycotted classes in our rage and disgust about something, and lived in tents on campus with peace symbols on them, smoking dope into the early morning. I was usually dressed as Chairman Mao and waved a red book which was actually a Yellow Pages book that I'd painted red. I was so militant I once went into a fancy restaurant and liberated the lobsters from the tank to set them free. Sadly, many of them were run over by passing trucks, but it was the thought. 'Stop cruelty to animals!' I shouted through a bullhorn, as I was splatted in lobster meat.

So why everyone feels so surprised by teens being difficult I do not know. My children are 'woosies' compared to me.

Understanding What's in the Teen Brain

Here, I'm only mentioning a few of the major areas that change most dramatically.

Amygdala Besides the hormonal changes, there's a whole redecoration going on in the brain. The amygdala, the motherboard of emotions, develops eighteen months sooner in girls, but the boys catch up and then they both have these mood swings that make a bipolar seem laidback. These emotional meltdowns means that your teen's limbic system is being flooded with uncontrollable emotions like a computer that's crashing from overload. If you start expressing anger, you'll only ignite his anger, and World War Three begins. You have to help him learn to cool down by staying attentive and calm and trying to get into his shoes.

Prefrontal Cortex The prefrontal cortex is still a work in progress at this stage, so isn't always working at maximum capacity. Sometimes it's capable of good decision-making and other times it's out of order and the teen goes emotionally berserk. You'll recognize that this has happened when, after a tirade of reasons why you're so unfair, your teen will slam into his room and play ear-shattering heavy metal while ripping his pillow to shreds. Don't worry: this is the typical teen brain finding its feet.

As a teen, the prefrontal cortex begins to link to other regions of the brain, and this integration finally creates self-awareness, empathy and the ability to think before you leap.

Brain Stem In the early teen years the primitive area is more active, so hot emotions, boiling away under the surface, can suddenly blow like a volcano, spraying lava on anyone nearby. As I said, your teen's prefrontal cortex is still under construction, so he has absolutely no means of being able to lasso in that temper. With a half-assed PFC, he's incapable of much empathy so has no interest in what anyone else is feeling. This is why parents are often treated like dirt. Chances are he's not mad at you, you just happen to be in the way. You may have just said, 'Anyone want a sandwich?' and he interpreted it as if you're implying he's an idiot who wouldn't know mayonnaise from a trouser press.

Hippocampus All this neural activity takes up energy, which explains why teenagers sleep thirty-seven hours in the day. When they finally wake up, they can't concentrate, because their hippocampus hasn't finished growing either, which makes it difficult to lay down long-term memory. You know how you repeat things over and over again and your teen forgets each time? This is why.

Chemicals Lacking any form of self-regulation, your teen isn't able to switch on his feel-good biochemicals – oxytocin, serotonin and dopamine to calm him in moments of crisis – to deal with his emotional hijacks. He can't manufacture endorphins (another feel-good chemical), which would turn off his adrenaline and would turn down the stress levels and the negative thoughts that come with them.

The Baddies I won't go on about cortisol, I've gone on enough, but this is what swamps teens, just like the rest of us, when we're stressed, freaked out and furious. More than a third of older teenagers suffer from sleeping and eating disorders. This is why mindfulness can really help with sleeplessness, worry about exams, anxious thoughts and anxiety, and eating disorders.

Serotonin Serotonin moderates your teen's impulsive behaviour and regulates his sleep patterns. This is why he sleeps such weird hours.

Dopamine Your teen needs just the right levels of dopamine to motivate him, but too much can tip him into addiction, depression or even into a physical disorder. He will start to take bigger and bigger risks because this stuff is so addictive. Each time he comes down from a buzz, he'll need another one.

Dopamine bumps up impulsive behaviour; there is no off button ... ever. This is a state called 'hyper-rationality' where he has no notion of worst-case scenarios; everything is for the kick and the thrill of the moment. Part of the reason you might give your teen such a hard time is because, deep down, you're jealous that he's having the time of his life and you aren't.

A Few Other Things Going On with Your Teen

Independence

Just as a baby animal will trot, leap and fly away from its parents soon after its birth, so will your teenager fly the coop to seek independence, which he'll need if he's ever going to be able to steer through the sharp rocks of life. He is bidding you farewell to explore the world on his own, to seek novelty, take risks, connect with peers, deal with jerks and finally realize that the phrase teens always come up with – 'It's not fair' – is actually true. The neocortex gets thicker at this stage, and this can be measured in brain imaging. The result of this is an increase in conscious awareness, which creates a sense of self. This self wants you the parent out of the picture, so you're gone, in the blink of an eye, from God status to something sticky on the bottom of your teen's shoe.

Bonding with Their Own Kind: Socially Connecting

The oxytocin teens receive from their reward system makes social connections the most important thing in their world. They want to be popular, to be accepted by a gang, no matter how many piercings or tattoos it takes. They perceive social rejection as a threat to their existence, so not being invited to the right party is worse than cystitis.

When kids hit their teens, if they're male they need to disengage from Mommy; if they're female they need to disengage from Daddy. The reason for this is that, as children, they are so in love with their parents that, if it weren't for this separation phase, they would want to marry them (*see* Oedipus). At this point, friends become far more important to teens than parents because, in the future, when Mommy and Daddy are in heaven, they are the ones who are going to protect and nurture them.

Creative Thinking

At some point, the teenager will find his parents boring and old-fashioned (go figure), which incites him to think more innovatively, inventing new ideas and concepts – anything so he doesn't have to end up like them. (He usually does but, as a teen, he's still aiming higher.) Rather than learning by rote as he did as a kid, he now argues and wants to try out everything. (It's exhausting.) This will go on until adulthood, when he's stuffed back into the box. Each generation feels they have to top the last one and come up with unique solutions to be able to survive an ever more complex world. Just as your old dial-a-number telephone has been replaced by an iPhone 208 and your hoover is now voice-activated.

Each generation thinks their parents have screwed up the world. The teen's job is to clean up his parents' mistakes and blame them for being selfish, greedy bastards who just think about themselves and are to blame for the world being a mess, the ice cap melting and the fact that there are no jobs or money because they've spent it all. (On these points, they're right on all fronts.)

Risk-taking

The biggest risk for a teen would be not taking a risk. We only progress because the latest generation always gets out there and throws caution to the wind while the old one watches television and dribbles. The teen's brain is now producing dopamine at break-neck speed, so now it's all about reward, no matter how dangerous the challenge. If your teen's friends are watching, he will take twice as many risks. The death rate of teens between fifteen and nineteen years of age is six times higher than that of children between ten and fourteen.

When I was seventeen, my friends and I hitch-hiked for twenty-seven hours to Mexico to go to a festival of the Punta Yaya (or something) we'd heard about. When we got there, an old, parched taco maker offered me a ladleful of mescal, which I think is the organic version of mescaline. I swallowed a mouthful and woke up three days later, lying in the street with a hoof mark on my face . . . I had missed the festival. I ended up (abandoned by my friends) taking a bus filled with peyote-crazed locals into the jungle on the

southern tip of Mexico. I had heard there was a community of hippies living there and wanted to find them. After four days' travelling on a three-wheeled bus with a chicken on my head, I found them. I stayed a month; meanwhile, my parents kept phoning my room mate at university and asking where I was. For a month she said I was in the shower. They sent out a red-light alert for me when they finally sussed that no one can get that clean, and on my return had me arrested.

There are, of course, downsides to risk-taking, like crashing the car into someone's living room and getting pregnant without being able to remember by whom.

Parenting a Teen Mindfully

If we start yelling at the kid who is having the meltdown, he'll only yell back and get more furious. If you can manage your emotions, you stand more of a chance that he can, too. By helping him deal with his cortisol overdrive (and yours), his prefrontal cortex can bloom and grow. The first thing to do is to learn to intentionally modify your tone of voice when you want to drive a point home rather than use the nagging, screechy voice I grew up with.

I tried to have my parents surgically removed from my mind, but I found it impossible. My inner critic to this day continues to have a Viennese accent whose pitch is a top F, like an air-raid siren that never turns off. This is why every organ in my body is always ready for the next Blitzkrieg. My parents didn't like it when I went my own crazy way, and the result was we never became close and I will never really know who they were as people. We rarely saw each other later in life and we were at war to the end. I feel it was their loss as well as mine. If they could have said, even once, that they might perhaps have been wrong about something, all would have been forgiven.

Be Mindful Yourself

If you as a parent are mindful, it's easier to make your child mindful. If you're playing mind games, acting out and having hissy fits, your teen will match you and sling it right back. If he just sits there and takes it, this could be an even bigger problem; either he's sitting on his rage, or he's shut down. You have to speak his language and see things through his eyes, rather than throw up your hands in frustration, insisting that he's speaking in tongues which you can't understand. You need to acknowledge that his risk-taking, his seeking of independence, the fact that he puts his friends above you, are all necessary parts of his natural development.

Don't start grinning insanely at him either: he can sense if your outside doesn't match up with what's going on inside you. A teen is a professional 'phoney' detective (*see Catcher in the Rye*).

Admit Your Mistakes

If you have let it rip in anger – which we've all done – after the dust has settled, say you're sorry and admit you aren't perfect. He already knows you're not, but it's good he knows you know. You don't want to get caught in the 'blame game', where you each retaliate with, 'It's your fault.' 'No, it's your fault.' 'No, it's your fault.' Your anger will fuel his, and it won't get you anywhere.

Empathize

When your teen comes home with a broken heart because he hasn't made the football team or has been rejected by someone he's fallen in love with, listen to him. Don't give advice, but empathize with the pain ... come on, you remember how much it hurt to be dumped, so share your horrible experiences with him. Teenagers love hearing that you, too, once suffered like they are now. The worse your experience, the happier your teen will feel. You'll become more like a human to him, instead of a Martian. If you try to understand him, he'll try to understand you. Don't lecture; be inquisitive, open and flexible rather than judgemental (teens hate being judged). He might even let you into his world and, as a bonus, he might let you see who he really is.

Never, *never* say, if you happen to be right about something, 'I told you I was right' or 'Why didn't you listen to me in the first place?' Try to hold back on overstating things, on hammering it home. If you as a parent can pull this off, you deserve the Victoria Cross. (I haven't got there yet; I go on and on and on.)

Compromise

Compromise is the key. You may have to let your teen keep his room like a bombsite if you want him to wash the dishes and change his pants once a month. This will not only make your life more bearable, but it will set your teen up to learn negotiation techniques for adulthood.

Make deals. Maybe give him time online if he matches

the time spent cleaning the kitchen. (I've tried to explain to my kids that I'm not a slave or a professional cleaning person, but they don't believe me.)

Communicate with Them

When you and your teen are about to come to blows, one of you should start to think about alternative strategies. It will probably be you, because you have a bigger prefrontal cortex and should be, in an ideal world, the more self-controlled one. From experiments I've done myself, screaming louder, getting sarcastic, threats and slamming out of the room don't really work well to resolve conflicts.

Awareness is everything, so try to notice when the reptile of rage is still in its infancy before it turns into the fully fledged Tyrannosaurus Rex. If you release it, your teen will, too, and now the argument becomes a blood sport. However long the 'It's your fault. No, it's your fault. No, it's yours . . .' goes on, both of you will lose. I know how good it feels to 'let it rip', but in the end your relationship is more damaged and now you're both flooded with cortisol, which I've established is not good for your health. You've poisoned your child and yourself in one swift battle.

If you can be aware of your rising fury before it boils over, or even in the early stages, you could try and say, 'I hear what you're saying, but I have to take a few minutes to think about all this and then I'll get back to you.' Now you can leave the room to take a breather, holding yourself back from putting a hole in the wall with your fist . . . or his head. (If you can do this, I bow before you.)

He may still be furious when you come back but, believe me, it's the only way you can both cool down. When you come back into the room, it won't help going back over the argument or why it happened, that will only ignite the fuse again or restart the mud-slinging. Try to get across (perhaps when the heat is down and you're getting along) the fact that part of the human condition is that we're still deeply primitive.

Let Your Teenager Teach You

Adults can learn a few tricks of the trade from teens, like living in the moment, finding novelty in things rather than doing the same old same old, hunting out new thrills and making more social connections. Some of us know that this is the route to happiness, which is why you see so many old people at Glastonbury. Hang out with teens, because sometimes it's way more fun than being with some of your old, boring peers.

Okay, Enough of Mrs Good Guy

Pick your battles. If you constantly nag your kids, they will eventually go deaf. If you keep your powder dry for the really unacceptable behaviour, your teen will understand that you really mean business when you lay down the law and will hear you loud and clear. When you do lay down the law, do it without using sarcasm, cynicism or criticism – he has enough of that inside his brain, directed at himself. Make sure the punishment fits the crime and don't infuse it with shame so that he feels humiliation.

Helping Him

If you notice your teen is swarming with dopamine and badly wants to take dangerous risks, buy him a punchbag, a tennis racquet, a jousting stick, an unbroken mustang (horse, not car) – anything to help him work off those hormones in a less detrimental way. Help him (if he wants help) to come up with a strategy to dump the dopamine.

So How Do You Teach Them Mindfulness?

Teaching mindfulness to teenagers ain't going to be a piece of cake, especially if you suggest it; as a parent, at this point you are an object of embarrassment; an untouchable.

Your teen might wonder why he would need to do such a bizarre and seemingly useless thing. If he refuses to do something that helps him self-regulate, tell him he'll be more popular, get better exam results without burning his brains out and be able to talk to the opposite sex without stuttering and sweating. Don't mention mindfulness unless he asks about it. For the moment, just plant the seeds of the fact that he can do something about feeling so out of control and being at the mercy of his mind and that by becoming aware of what his mind is up to he'll be able to lower his own stress levels.

Once those teenage years kick in and rebelling becomes the *mode du jour*, the question many parents ask me is how do you get your teen to practise or even comprehend mindfulness when his brain is like a bucking bronco? You're dealing with a person who won't get off his Twitter machine or the Book of Face. He doesn't want to know about some technique that steadies his mind – why ruin a good time?

Exercise: Name It to Tame It

Maybe you could suggest that your teen could try to take his emotional temperature once in a while, even if it's just by a few degrees. As the feelings start to heat up, suggest that maybe he could label them. He doesn't have to tell you what they are, he can write them down or maybe say them to himself. Many teenagers may only know a few words that describe feelings; I know this because when I asked my teenage kids how they were, they responded with either 'okay' or 'crap'. It might be helpful to give them a more extensive list of vocab. There are about five thousand words to describe emotions, so they can expand their repertoire by quite a bit.

Explain that when he gives a simple, one-word label to feelings, especially the hot ones, he'll avoid stoking up the rumination about why he feels what he feels. A label means he's noticed, but he doesn't have to interpret it.

You can also tell your teen about re-routing the hot emotion from the mind to the sense of it in the body. Tell him that all feelings are okay: it's part of being human, we all have them – even the feeling of wanting to kill your parents. (The important thing might be to learn not to act on it.)

Here's an exercise you could try.

Make two circles out of cardboard and draw slices on them like a pizza. On each slice write down an emotion, for example, anger, boredom, loneliness or excitement. And a few of the 4,966 others. Stick the two circles on the fridge and have your teen put a magnet on the word that matches his mood. You, as a parent, put your magnet on your emotion on the circle. This gives you both a clear idea of your weather conditions within; what you're feeling in that moment.

When you make your mood clear, your teen can understand where you are emotionally and can therefore better adjust his dials to deal with you. If you see that his magnet is on rage, walk away; if it's on joy, bring out the confetti.

Exercise: Show Them Their Brains and How They Work

Use a drawing of the brain to demonstrate what happens during an amygdala hijack and the cortisol and adrenaline explosion that goes with it. Let your teen know that it's hard for all of us to stop the flow once we erupt. Explain about the brain stem, how it has a mind of its own and can make all of us (not just teens) act crazy and impulsive.

Show him how the prefrontal cortex works, but explain that his is still developing. (Make sure he knows that it's nothing personal or something he's done wrong – all teens have PFCs in development.)

Exercise: Picture It

When your teen starts to lose it, he can try to visualize something or someone that makes him happy. Some examples might be hanging with his homies (how young and cool am I?); looking at a photo of his best friend, a holiday snap or his cat (my daughter loves baby seals; if she sees a photo she immediately goes all gooey); kicking something (not a person); calling a friend; jogging/ playing a musical instrument loudly (drums are good, but not at home, please).

It's good if he understands that this exercise isn't to put a stop to his feelings but that, by learning how his brain works and what he can do to deal with those turbulent emotions, he'll be better able to deal with some of the horrors and stresses of being a teen. Here are just a few of the things that might be disturbing him: exam results; low self-esteem; feeling not good enough; feeling that he doesn't look good enough; being made to feel like a dweeb; being left out; being bullied; being laughed at; not knowing what to do about sex/ drugs/ drink; not fitting in; standing out; feeling alone and anxious; feeling under pressure from parents/ teachers/ everyone; pimples; the future . . .

When your teen imagines what happens when he self-regulates, it actually starts to happen. Hopefully, some-day, he might be able to say, 'Oh, that's an amygdala hijack I'm having.' Or 'Wow, that was a seriously bad cortisol rush.' This way, he can watch how his emotions work rather than just expressing them. The idea behind all this is that he will eventually tune into his emotions and be able to sense his internal weather conditions. Let him come up with his own solutions as to how to regulate his emotions so the power is all his.

9

Mindfulness and Me

For the ending of the book, I thought I'd go to the University of Bangor in Wales, a centre for mindfulness research, and have my brain scanned before and after a week-long retreat, with no Wi-Fi and seven hours of meditation a day. (I don't know which sounds worse.) I figured that, if I'm writing this book about mindfulness, I might as well see if it delivers what it says on the label . . . and what better way than to use me as the guinea pig? Sharon Hadley, who is the manager of the Centre of Mindfulness, Research and Practice, arranged everything, from my brain scans to fixing me up with a retreat.

I arrive at the neuroscience building at the university and am led to the room with the brain scanner in it. It's a breath-taking moment when you look at a piece of machinery that lets you see the activity in every part of your brain by means of a piece of software that produces colour pictures of who you are in 3D. I am introduced to Paul Mullins (Director of the Bangor NeuroImaging Unit at the School of Psychology and Senior MRI Physicist), who has taken time off from his sabbatical to come and do the brain scans. (Thank you, Paul.) He takes me through a questionnaire that asks things like, 'If we find something "unusual", do you want to be told?' Who else would they tell? Other questions: 'Have you ever been in a scanner before?' and 'How are you in enclosed spaces?'

I tell Paul that I love being in a scanner; I lived in one in Glastonbury (no laugh from him). Then comes the disclaimer, which says that, if anything happened to me, I wouldn't blame them. He tells me no one will ever know that this is my brain; the scan will be completely anonymous. I'm thinking, 'Why would I care? It's me in there. I've been on TV, what's the big secret?' Like they're going to see my mind and report me to the thought police?

Paul asks if I have any metal anywhere in my body, because the MRI scanner has a magnet strong enough to suck a fridge across Poland. He asks if I'm wearing an underwired bra. When I inquire why this is relevant, he says I wouldn't want to know. (Later in the day I meet someone in the building who tells me horror stories of people being crushed in the scanner by metal objects that have been sucked in; a metal chair once got dragged in and killed the person in the scanner. Imagine that. They're in there, worrying about a brain tumour, and next thing they're killed by a chair?)

Anyway, after the metal removal, I lie down on the track, wrapped in a blanket, have a helmet lowered over my face and, with a push of a button, I'm rolled into the open cave of a coffin-like structure. They ask if I want to use mirrors so I can see the staff through the glass looking at the monitors. Of course I do: I want to register the expression on their faces when they see the white light in my brain. (Secretly, I've always imagined that, beneath the mess, I'm the 'chosen one'.) So Paul says he's ready, and the drilling sounds starts, which he's warned me about. It sounds like someone's excavating a building . . . and I'm the building. I'm thinking, 'This equipment costs millions and they couldn't find a way to make it quiet?' I'm looking at them through my mirror and I see them talking to each other and laughing like they're discussing the football results. My brain is on that screen; they're looking at the live action of my memories, my thoughts, hopes, dreams, happiness, despair . . . my everything – and they're talking about what's for lunch? After an hour of watching them chat without seeing any sign of amazement on their faces that I'm the next messiah, I get up, and there on the monitor is my brain in living colour . . . and it's beautiful. It's all lit up like a neon fish with trillions of fluorescent wires, and I can see it from all angles. It's so amazing I'm thinking I could sell it at the Saatchi gallery . . . or at least on eBay. Then I see on the scan what looks like thousands of X-rays of all those regions in the brain that a brain's supposed to have. Thank God, there aren't any empty, blank spaces.

Then Paul says the words that everyone dreads: he's spotted an 'abnormality'. I've imagined these moments, as a professional hypochondriac, for most of my life so, because I am well-rehearsed, I have almost no reaction. He says there are things on some of the images and he doesn't know what they are (I, of course, conclude that he's lying), and do I want a neurologist to check it out? Duh. Yes!!!

After retrieving all my metal, and in a glaze of shock, off I go to another room, to have an EEG. This is the one where they put wires all over your head. This procedure electronically shows your neural activity as it happens. Dr Dusana Dorjee, who has a PhD in cognitive neuroscience and is a leading researcher at the Centre for Mindfulness Research and Practice, is doing the procedures. After a shower cap with holes has been placed snugly on my head, she sets me three exercises. She asks me to meditate for two minutes, focusing on my breath. Then, for another two minutes, I should let my mind wander and allow myself to ruminate, getting hooked on the thoughts as they come in. In the third exercise she asks me to mind-wander but not to get caught up in the stories, to let my thoughts come and go without me trying to analyse them. (This is called open attention.)

After this, she asks me to do all three exercises again but, this time, two photos will come up on a monitor and I have to hit the left button if the photos are similar and the right one if they're different. She wants to see whether, when someone is in a meditative state, they react less strongly to disturbing images. The first pair is a plane flying and a plane crashed on the ground, so I hit the left button for similar. The next couple are a shark and an ironing board. (I know those are different.) Then a tarantula and a golf club. I don't think any of the photos disturbed me; I only get riled when I get it wrong and I push the similar button when I mean to push the one for different. I'm imagining I'm on some TV game show and I have to win at all costs; I am in full competitive mode . . . with myself. (This is so typical.)

Later that day, I'm driven to the hotel I'll be staying at, where, in the lobby, a group of locals are teaching Welsh dancing. The women are wearing top hats like Abraham Lincoln's and old Puritan dresses with aprons, and playing violins and accordions. I'm grabbed by a man wearing something even weirder who twirls me in circles; just circles. How can this be Welsh dancing when it's just circles? I go along with it. I'm thinking this must be the effect of whatever the abnormality is on my brain.

Day One

The following day, I'm taken off to the Trigonos Retreat Centre, which is on a lake somewhere in the back hills of Wales; it's the beginning of August, and it's winter. As soon as I get there, I realize I'm sick to my stomach and have to lie down. This could be because I've found out about the daily schedule, which is getting up at 7 a.m. and meditating, breakfast between eight and nine, then nine to twelve is meditating (half an hour sitting meditation, half an hour walking meditation, then sitting again, then a tea break; then sitting meditation for a half an hour, then walking half an hour). Then it's lunch. Between three and six it's the same thing: sitting and walking while meditating for three hours. Then dinner and then sitting, and at 9 p.m. sleeping . . . and all of this in *silence*.

This is mental boot-camp; if anyone thinks it's just new-agey fluff, go try it yourself. So, for the first day, I am nauseous. I sit in silence (in sickness) and hope I don't throw up. Afterwards – and I don't know how I got there – I hit that bed and am unconscious until the next morning. That first night I dream that Obama is cleaning a glass coffee table while making a wonderful speech about world peace.

Day Two

I get up when my phone alarm goes at 6.57 a.m. for my seven o'clock meditation (I like to cut it close for adrenaline-rush reasons, even in a retreat). So I scramble into the large meditation room, where people are already sitting, some wrapped in shawls in Buddha positions, some on cushions and some on the latest in meditation accoutrements for your bum: a zafu (Google it; it's a cushion). I took to a chair, just to rebel.

Our retreat is led by two women who I would categorize under the heading 'Earth Mothers'; hair awry, and I think one of them is wearing those rubber clogs with holes like shower mats (which I imagine are useful if you're in a flood).

And I'm thinking they're going to start with those soft, feathery voices you get in healing centres where they gently rub warmed-up ylang-ylang oil on to your central-line meridian. When I speak to one of the women, Jody Mardula, the ex-director of the Centre for Mindfulness Research and Practice, I realize I am wrong. I tell her about the 'abnormality' on my brain and that I might be a little preoccupied during the retreat. I expect her to give me a mug of bark juice but nope, she proceeds to tell me in a light-hearted manner how she had to retire as director about five years ago due to a brain haemorrhage.

She tells me, only because I push her, that she had suddenly felt a cold waterfall going down the back of her head and had then passed out with the pain. She says it was like a tsunami of blood flowing under her scalp down to her neck. When she woke up, she says she felt like her memories had been washed away in the devastation; some were buried under collapsed buildings and some were sticking out of the mud. She had no memory of who she was or what she was doing in the hospital (and I had started this conversation feeling sorry for myself). After a few weeks she was so constrained by all the wires keeping her alive she could only move her right hand, so she'd do body scans and concentrate, in a kind of mindfulness exercise, on the feeling of where her hand contacted the bed sheet, grounding herself to a physical sensation. Later, once she could move the other hand, she would focus on the feeling of both hands where they contacted each other. This, she said, sharpened her ability to pay attention and bring her mind back into focus when it got lost in the pain.

Months later, she got better, but she never regained her old self so she had to create a new one. Later, others tell me that Jody (when she was younger) used to hitch-hike alone across countries and once lived on a rooftop in Paris, where she was known for wild parties. They said that, even when she was on walking sticks during her recovery, she asked some kids who were sliding down a snow-covered mountain on bits of cardboard if she could try it. She put her sticks on her lap and, to their amazement, took off down the slope.

She tells me that her experience wasn't all bad (can you believe someone can say that?), that when she created this new self, she no longer had any critical voices in her head telling her she wasn't good enough, that she wasn't qualified to hold her job. Nowadays, she just accepts what she is and seems at peace with it all, like it's the most natural thing on earth to lose your memory. She remembers her daughter, and that's enough for her. So there's a lesson: I thought she was a lightweight, and she turns out to be more evolved than almost anyone I've ever met.

Day Three

I'm not having the greatest time. When you sit and meditate for a long time, your internal voice is screaming for it to end and begging for the *ting ting* that signifies the sitting is over.

And then it's over and you have to go straight into the walking meditation, where you walk one way for about ten feet and then back the other way. The idea is that you try to focus on where your feet touch the ground so that when your mind wanders you take your attention back to one of your feet and feel the next step . . . then your mind goes to some phone call you forgot to return two years ago . . . then you send your focus back to your foot and move to the other one. Gradually, as agonizing as it is to watch your mind play every trick in the book to get you back to thinking what it wants to think about, you start to see the point of all this. You're taking your focus by the horns and using the sense of your feet as an anchor to come back to when your mind snares you. While some of us are doing the slow walking outside, a helicopter flies over and I imagine the pilot looking down and thinking he is watching *The Night of the Living Dead*.

After sitting, walking, sitting, finally there's a *ting* to have lunch. Everyone waits in the queue, no one pushes, everyone's considerate – opening doors for you, handing you a cup. I like all these people, mostly because I don't have to talk to any of them. Your eyes never meet because, as you don't have anything to say, there's no reason to look at each other. You save so much energy when you don't have to say, 'Thank you' or 'Sorry' all the time; it's such a relief. All I have to do is focus in on what I'm eating.

Today I fall in love with a digestive biscuit. I've had them before . . . but not like this. I have one bite and I almost tip off my chair with the burst of salt and sugar and crunchiness; it's perfect. I never want it to end. You start to slow down your chewing and stop thinking about taking another bite before you've even swallowed what's in your mouth (my usual mode of eating). You savour the moment because the experience is so poignant: you let the taste, better than anything a five-star restaurant could offer, become your only focus of attention; all thoughts subside. I end up wrapping up the other half of the biscuit in a napkin, and save it, in my shoe, for a special occasion. And then the *ting* happens to indicate that lunch is over and, like in a zombie film, we all go back into the room to our zafu – or chair, in my case.

I start nodding off while I'm sitting on my chair, thinking that time is going so slowly but even here it still moves on. (I think I am being very profound.)

By now I am wearing my pyjama bottoms and an old moth-eaten felt jacket (it was freezing, so I had to borrow it – and wellies to match), because when no one looks at you, you don't look at you either. (I didn't see a mirror the whole time – another relief.) I notice that I'm starting to slow down, and that frightens me, like I'm going to grind to a halt and end up a statue. When we do the walking meditation, I can barely lift my feet; my whole body is like a dead weight and I haul it like I'm carrying a dead elephant. I feel like my grandmother in her last days, dragging herself around the house like a pool cleaner.

During the time we're there, we're allowed a fifteen-minute meeting with one of the teachers to tell them what's on our silent minds. So I go to see Jody to tell her that I feel really old and am terrified I'm going to end up eating scones with other old people and pottering around the garden for fun. I feel my life will end shortly.

Then she tells me she's seventy (so much for my problems) and asks what I've learnt so far. I tell her that I feel like I've freed myself from the idea I held when I was younger that I was carrying poison and it was just a matter of time before people would cotton on that something was deeply bad about me and fire me, throw me out or just dump me. I tell her I don't feel that way any more – that slate is wiped clean – but that I'm still narcissistic; and she says, 'Who isn't?' I mention again how frightened I am that I might lose my memory. (I say this to a woman who has. Sensitive or what?) She said I should stop catastrophizing . . . no one ever said I was going to lose my memory. She has a point. I tell her, even though we're supposed to be focused on ourselves, that I'm starting to go back to my old ways: I'm starting to zero in on people in the group who I don't like. Remember: they're silent – so where am I getting my information? I can't stand one person because he breathes too loudly, or another one who sits with his eyes shut even after the *ting* goes indicating the session is finished . . . like he's in nirvana, wearing Tibetan socks and a dot on his head, and I'm furious at one woman who eats with her mouth open.

Jody says that, when she's on a silent retreat, in her mind she kills a few people, marries a few and then divorces some. She tells me she likes me and that she doesn't feel that way about everyone, and I tell her the same. New best friend.

I go back to . . . what else? Sitting . . . it never ends. I start counting how many more hours are left until I can go home. I feel my mind's like a spoiled brat: it wants to eat, to sleep, to go to France, it wants the sleeting rain to stop (it's August – what's wrong with this country?) – but I'm getting more than a slight inkling about the effect this mindfulness lark might be having. From this endless exercise, I can actually feel the muscle of my attention growing from a puny little bump to something quite powerful; I'm able to keep my attention on a particular thing for a longer period than I normally could. The voices don't stop, but because I have stopped trying to stop them (or wishing that they were more profound) they're getting less vitriolic. I'm becoming less frightened that I might not be as special as I think I am. My ego is starting to do a striptease.

(Only days ago, in the brain scanner, I thought my brain was a golden orb of enlightenment.) None of us wants to look into our mind and discover that we're just simple folk and that we're no different from each other under our armour. We are all delusional if we think we're above the herd; we're all just people trying to scratch out some kind of a life. If we demand too much of ourselves, life isn't fun and we make ourselves ill, so why do that? I've always wondered why I am such a slave driver to myself? I usually can't think without pushing my mind to heights it can't reach – like a mother who pushes her child until he goes over the edge. Why can't I just leave me alone? I realize I might be so stressed in life because I'm always trying to improve myself, when it's okay just to be me, with these plain, vanilla thoughts. And as I sit there and the thoughts arise, it's as if they're rising like sediment from the bottom of a pail of clear water. Each time one disengages from the bottom, the water below gets clearer.

As I start to get off my own back, I notice that all this self-punishment for not doing enough is starting to go; I can even feel the muscles in my face moving towards a smile. I'm beginning to be able to stand back and observe my thoughts and, when I get even a trace of a negative thought or the first scent of rumination, I can re-route my focus from my head into my body, where I can sensually investigate it rather than agonize about it. I've always said that, with depression, it's impossible to know when it's coming, because you don't have a spare brain to assess whether there's something wrong, like you could with a lost finger or a lump. So I know I can't get a warning in words that it's coming, as in, 'Oh, I'm getting depression. What should I do about it?' But from all this practising, this bulking up of my insula, I know I'll be able to *sense* it coming. I won't feel so unaware, so helpless, next time; I understand now that the two statements 'There is sadness' and 'I am sad' are different. (It's part of me, not the whole of me.)

I do my walking meditation this afternoon outside by the stream, which, I notice, always burbles . . . except when I'm not listening. I play with that idea, noticing the difference when I'm tuned out to when I'm tuned in, and I start to experiment, choosing where to focus my attention, on the noise of the wind a mile away or on an insect up close? Why do I miss so much in my life? I don't remember ever hearing the wind in London. All these years and I missed out on the wind, which is all I can hear here, besides the sound of the stream going over rocks into little waterfalls, which I can stare at for more than my normal ten-second limit. I smell a rose (making sure no one is looking) and decide to do my walking up and down near it so that, when the wind is right, I can get smacked in the face by that smell. Every time I pass it, I get a hit. The next day, the rose is dead and there's no smell. I think there's a lesson in there . . . I'm not sure what. No, I know: the lesson is that all things die, so don't depend on them. (Profound or what?)

Now that I know I'm in charge of pulling focus, I decide at dinner to watch a particular sheep on the faraway mountain and then throw my focus on to a daddy-long-legs on the windowsill. The insect captures my attention for so long I think we're starting a relationship. Who knew that daddy-long-legs were so fascinating? If you reach out to touch one of its legs it senses you and moves away, using these two hair-like antennas. They feel around like a blind person using a white stick. They're agile and can walk on anything, sideways and upside down. (I do experiments.)

That night at dinner I fall in love with a potato. (I've moved on from the digestive.) I couldn't believe that it could taste so sweet and crunchy and then so fluffy – it had everything going for it. I go into the kitchen and break my silence, demanding to know how they had cooked the potato. The chef shows me a potato and some Tesco olive oil. I don't get it: I have eaten potatoes in my life, but never on this level. Again, I'm wanting another one while I still have one in my mouth, and I think, 'Yup, this is how I live my life.'

Day Four

I'm still not good at getting up without leaping from my bed from some emergency happening in my dream; last night it was being gunned down by snapping turtles. (Good luck with that one, Freud.) Now awake, I fill the bathtub; I never realized the difference in the feel of hot water as opposed to cold. Downstairs, I join the others for some t'ai chi-type exercises. I'm smirking to myself, thinking that these are pathetic moves, lifting my arms up and down, slowly. I'm a person who can do push-ups, for God's sake; I can do downward dog for hours on end. So I start to lift both arms up really slowly . . . and find I can't. It's just too exhausting to lift my own arms. You can imagine the mental berating I'm giving myself for being such a wimp, but I do something I've almost never done in my life: I give up and just lift one arm . . . halfway.

At breakfast, where the taste of a raisin in my cereal leaves me breathless, I start trying to figure out why I feel so flat-lined (not depressed – this is something else, more dreamy, not scary). I realize that my amygdala has been out of commission since day one because there's nothing in here that's frightening. I can trust everyone; they can't hurt me when they're not speaking, and probably wouldn't if they could. This is what it's like when I'm not on the lookout for trouble. At this moment, I'm not really worried about anything; even the fear of not finishing this book has disappeared.

This afternoon we break the silence when the teachers ask us to give an update of what's happening in our minds. One woman says she can't stop planning things (she does it for a living); early in the day, she plans which cushion she's going to sit on and even what she's going to focus on in her body. Another woman says she thinks that everything she does is stupid and knows that everyone else thinks she's stupid. (She isn't, but I can't tell her that in my silence.) One guy says he keeps hunting around for some problem because, in life, that's what he is, a problem-solver, so without a problem to solve he feels empty. He then tries to solve the problem of the woman who says she's stupid. Jody tells him to stop it. She says, when you think you're being empathetic, you're actually just avoiding your own issues. It's more your need to help than theirs to be helped. Also, if you keep trying to help others you get something called empathy fatigue. People need you to hear them clearly if you want to help them, not be lost in how bad you feel for them.

The talking ends, and I go back to . . . guess what? . . . sitting. I'm caught by the sound of two dogs barking in the distance. One is a baritone – I'm guessing he's a Great Dane; the other a small, snippy, yappy dog. I get transfixed listening to them, noticing that they aren't being hostile, as I would have assumed in the past, they're just having a dog conversation. They stop, and I find myself missing their noise. When my thoughts start pouring into my head, I try to hear them as if they're like the sound of dogs barking; some are loud, some soft, some frantic, some funny. This is working because the barking is untranslatable so I can't get caught up in it. I'm barking to myself. If I could see my thoughts like this all the time I wouldn't be so screwed up. I should start marketing my new practice, Barking-Based Cognitive Therapy (BBCT).

Day Five

I woke up a few times during the night, as I routinely do at home; usually, it takes me a long time to get back to sleep, if I ever do. Last night was different. When I woke, at about 3 a.m., I tried to do what I'm doing seven hours each day: to focus on my breath and, when my thoughts take over, just bring it back. I also noticed the moment that the images in my mind became unreal, indicating I was starting to dream, even though I was conscious. I could tell because someone in my mind started to grow starfish arms and legs, and I remember thinking, 'That can't happen in real life, this must be the beginning of dreaming' . . . and then I drifted off.

At the first meditation of the morning I notice that my mind is quietening down. It feels like I have taut banjo strings across my stomach which now are ripping apart with a *ping*. The sick feeling I had on my first day is gone and has been replaced by a tranquil kind of tingling under my ribs which then travels up my left side to the side of my head. When the *ting ting* sounds (get this), I want to stay sitting. This has never happened before. I realize I am not trying to correct my posture or my breathing but am just completely settled, at home in my body, with no urge to get up. The 'I want' button is switched off, so I can clearly hear the noises around me. I can't hear the dogs, but the wind's howling in all octaves and the door's open so it hits my face and feels like someone is breathing into me. I start to get little whispers of 'This must mean I'm doing really well. I am so getting this right. Look at me, everyone, I'm at the top of the class.' I catch myself doing this and, for the first time, I don't get out the whip; I'm amused.

After a while, because my stomach is flashing for food, I

go to breakfast and find that I'm not so interested in eating but instead am intentionally throwing my focus away from things close up to those far away, as if I am using binoculars. I throw my focus wide and watch the mountains, and the clouds casting light over them like a wave. During walking meditation I find I can more easily throw my focus from a leaf to the whole tree, then up to the sky and then back to a bee with its sucker sucking on a purple flower. This place is like a paradise (even though it is still cold), and I decide that if the problem with the white spots in my brain means that I lose my memory, if I can just experience getting this full-frontal hit of my senses and absorb completely what's in front of my eyes for the rest of my life, I might be okay with it. I hope if my mind does go I remember who my friends and family are but, otherwise, this focusing on the details of things around me, without flitting off to the next thing, is perfect.

Later, I get an image that letting all these thoughts drift around me is like swimming in a lake. It can be clear and icy or a murky soup, but it has nothing to do with me: I'm not the water, I'm just the swimmer. As I swim, I can just look around, not searching for problems like dead coral reefs or a shark. I can just enjoy myself in it.

The dogs bark again tonight, I love the sound and wonder where they are. When I go back to real life I'm going to have to find my old personality and somehow put it on again.

Day Six

This morning I go to my chair as if it is a long-lost friend that I want to sit on for ever. I have that tingly feeling again and am so grateful that I have no pain anywhere in my body and can feel all this new energy. Hurrah! I'm not that old. My thoughts are quieter than usual, and when they do come I treat them like a parent telling her kids to go to sleep because it's late. I feel no past or future, just this moment, listening to this stream of consciousness like I'm listening to the stream outside. I go to breakfast here for the last time and notice some of the people, and drift right back to judging them.

The Buddha guy is still in a trance with his eyes closed, smelling his porridge, and I think, 'What a wanker,' but I figure that's part of who I am. I don't have to tell him he's a wanker; I can just think it. A few of us just sit and look out of the window like there's a big, box-office blockbuster showing there. We're all entranced by a black-and-white bird that has just landed, the tractor in the distance and the sheep that keep moving (I never notice them doing it, but they're always in a new spot). It's amazing; I can tell that no one wants to be anywhere else but here, watching. I take one last digestive but only eat half because I have to go outside to smell that rose . . . it's dead, but I'm just checking. I say good-bye to the dogs that I never met. I don't want all this to end . . . but it will and does . . . everything does.

(In case some of you out there are wondering what the abnormalities on my brain were, I had to have another brain scan in London when I got back and was told by a neurologist that what I had was not of any relevance. So it all ended happily . . . or as happy as we can get.)

On this last day I returned to Bangor University, where Dr Dusana Dorjee performed the EEG test on me again. Dr Dusana is a very brilliant academic and neuroscientist; I'm going to give you my humble translation of her research, which you'll find in the appendices at the back of this book.

This experiment was looking at the evidence of the effects of mindfulness on the self-regulation of emotions. Before the retreat, when I was shown the negative photos, for example, the plane crash, a destitute child, someone at gunpoint, I reacted with a high emotional response. I didn't feel it, but the EEG picks up the electrical activation of the neurons, so it shows what I'm not aware of. The heightened reaction (shown in the black bar in the chart on p. 237) reflects an amygdala hijack with the cascades of cortisol and adrenaline that accompany it. This reaction happened in spite of the fact that, at the time, I was asked to send my attention to my breathing. After the retreat, when shown the same negative pictures while again focusing on my breath, the results indicated that I was hardly emotionally affected at all and therefore had successfully self-regulated my responses.

Dr Dusana said that, in order for this type of experiment to have been completely valid, it would have had to involve a greater number of people, along with a control group.

I phoned Mark Williams (co-founder of MBCT) with news of the positive results and told him, to his amusement, that, had they found that mindfulness had no effect on me, I would have demanded my money back from Oxford and, as he was my professor, it wouldn't have looked good for him. I'd think, 'All those hours of practice, and for what? I could have been learning salsa.'

There are people who say that a scan doesn't really reveal how we feel subjectively and that all this neuroscientific experimentation tells us nothing about how we really think; your scan could show abnormalities, while you feel great.

Willem Kuyken (Professor of Clinical Psychology at the University of Oxford and Director of the Oxford University mindfulness centre) writes that 'the neuroscience of mindfulness is promising (in so far as it shows benefits for clinical disorders and generating healthier minds) but it's still in its infancy. Though brain scanning is an incredible technology right now, it's like looking at the galaxy through a limited telescope.' Whether you agree or not, irrespective of the results, I feel different in my body and in my mind. I don't think you can write a book like this and not be affected by being so immersed in this practice.

I feel a little sad that I'm no longer so gripped by the persona I worked so hard to create. It got me through. In the past, I could fool myself into thinking what I was doing or who I was doing it with was important to my life. I feel now like I've busted myself; I see my motivations much more clearly. Sometimes, for example, I was using people to distract me from feeling so false and pointless.

I still have the same hot emotional triggers – I don't think they ever go – but they're much fainter; I can watch them coming down the pipeline and remember that they're just triggers, not facts.

I don't know if or when I'll have another depression, but I don't live in fear of it, so I'm reducing my medication with the condition that, if I'm not in the percentage of people who can successfully come off them, I won't think it's because I'm a failure. I've lost my fear of being alone. I like being alone these days and listening into my thoughts rather than running from them by being eternally busy. My thoughts aren't as bad as I thought; sometimes they're actually fun to be around. So yes, all this changed me. For now, I can't predict what happens next but, in this moment, I feel awake.

Appendices

Changes in Brain Reactivity to Negative Pictures After a Mindfulness Retreat

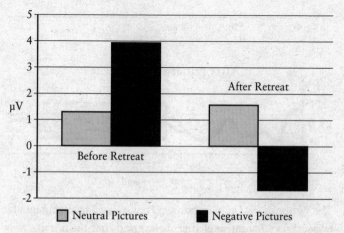

The figure shows the magnitude of brain responses (event-related potentials) to neutral and negative pictures before and after the mindfulness retreat with smaller responses to negative pictures after the retreat.

Below is a graph of my reactions to neutral and negative pictures when I'm focused on my breathing before and after the mindfulness retreat.

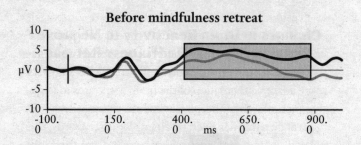

Before mindfulness retreat

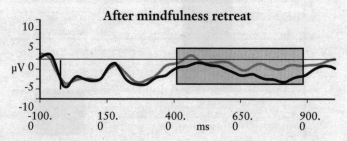

After mindfulness retreat

The figure shows brain responses (event-related brain potentials) to neutral and negative pictures before and after the mindfulness retreat. The highlighted area is the late positive potential (LPP) sensitive to regulation of emotions.

This is how they summed me up:

In our analyses, we were looking at a brain index (event-related brain potential, which is called the late positive potential (LPP)), which is sensitive to how effectively we are able to regulate emotions. Lower magnitude of this brain index suggests better ability to regulate emotions (e.g., Hajcak, 2006). In this study, we have compared the brain's responses to negative (of medium intensity) and neutral pictures while the participants were asked to meditate (to focus on their breath and to perceive whatever arises in their mind as fleeting, temporary experience). When comparing Ruby's results before and after a five-day retreat, we have found a decrease in the brain responses to negative pictures, but not to neutral pictures. This suggests more adaptive regulation of the brain responses to negative pictures after the retreat, while the sensitivity to neutral pictures has been retained. In other words, the effect did not seem to be simply due to 'de-sensitization' to the pictures after seeing the same pictures the second time, which often happens with repetition. These results seem to align with the findings from the only published study so far showing links between modulation of this brain index and mindfulness (Brown et al., 2012). In that study it has been found that higher levels of mindfulness disposition are associated with lower magnitude of this brain index. However, it is important to remember that the current comparison was only for one person tested before and after a retreat. To provide conclusive, rigorous results we would need to test a group of participants before and after a retreat and also control for the repetition effect by comparing the results of the retreat group to the changes in a group which did not engage in the retreat or engaged in a different activity.

References:

Brown, K. W., Goodman, R. J. & Inzlicht, M. (2012), 'Dispositional Mindfulness and the Attenuation of Neural

Responses to Emotional Stimuli', *Social Cognitive and Affective Neuroscience*, 8, Jan. 2013, (1) 93–9.

Hajcak, G. & Nieuwenhuis, S. (2006), 'Reappraisal Modulates the Electrocortical Response to Unpleasant Pictures', *Cognitive, Affective, & Behavioral Neuroscience*, 6 (4), 291–7.

'Investigating the Impact of Mindfulness Training on Adolescents' Attention and Emotion Regulation'

by Kevanne Sanger & Dusana Dorjee, PhD, Centre for Mindfulness Research and Practice, School of Psychology, Bangor University Mindful Brain Lab (http://mindfulbrain.bangor.ac.uk)

The aim of this project was to investigate changes in brain functioning resulting from mindfulness training delivered as part of the regular school curriculum to sixth-form students (aged sixteen to eighteen years). The study involved students from four schools in North Wales. School teachers in two schools delivered an eight-week mindfulness course to their students and we measured changes in brain activity patterns, questionnaire responses, and also number of GP visits before and after the course. Students from the other two (control) schools were tested at the same time for points for comparison; they continued with their school curriculum as usual and received mindfulness training when the assessments were completed. The brain responses were measured as brain wave patterns in two computer-based tasks. The first task assessed attention, with brain responses recorded to shapes displayed rarely or frequently. The second task measured brain responses to happy, sad and neutral faces displayed on the computer and assessed emotion processing and emotion regulation.

The results were encouraging, showing that the sixth-formers were better able to stop responses to shapes which were irrelevant to the attention task and distracting. This is important for maintaining attention focus. In the emotion task, students who received mindfulness training processed the emotions in faces more fully than students not trained in mindfulness. In fact, lower magnitude of brain responses to the emotional faces was seen over time in the group without mindfulness training. The questionnaire results also showed benefits: with mind-wandering increasing in the control group of students, but not in the mindfulness group, and well-being increasing in the training group. Moreover, students who had received mindfulness training reported fewer visits to their GP for mental health reasons, e.g. stress or sleep problems, after mindfulness training. Taken together, these results suggest that mindfulness training might increase adolescents' ability to remain focused on a task, and inhibit responding to distracting information. It can also have a positive effect on adolescent well-being, and encourage their openness to perceiving emotions in others.

Mindfulness with Primary-school Children

Researchers at the Centre for Mindfulness Research and Practice in the School of Psychology at Bangor University (Vickery & Dorjee, 2015) recently conducted the first study on mindfulness with primary-school children in the UK context. In this research, children from years 3 and 4 in one school received mindfulness training and their results were compared to those of children in the same years in two other schools which did not teach mindfulness (these two schools were offered mindfulness training after the completion of the assessments). The mindfulness training was delivered as part of the regular PSE curriculum by the children's own schoolteachers, who were trained in mindfulness six months earlier. The evaluations primarily focused on changes in emotional well-being of children and changes in metacognition – children's ability to notice and regulate their behaviour. Aspects of emotional well-being, such as positive and negative affect and emotional awareness, were evaluated in questionnaires filled in by the children. Metacognition was assessed through questionnaires completed by the children's teachers and parents. The children were assessed before the start of the mindfulness training, right after they had completed the training and three months after completion of the mindfulness training (with metacognition evaluated only before the training and three months after training). The researchers also evaluated how much children enjoyed practising mindfulness in school.

The results showed that most children (76 per cent) liked practising mindfulness in school, which is higher acceptability than most newly introduced subjects, with typical acceptability of about 50 per cent. There were also significant decreases in negative affect of children three months after the training and teachers reported significant improvements in children's metacognition. Parents did not report significant changes in children's metacognition. In some, most of the changes were found three months after the training, which is likely due to the mindfulness training first enhancing awareness and cognitive abilities of children and this then having an impact on their ability to self-regulate emotions. It is also possible that questionnaire measures are not sensitive enough to detect more subtle changes in children's attention abilities and emotion processing. Indeed, further studies conducted at Bangor with children from the same schools using brain-wave-derived markers suggested improved efficiency of attention after the mindfulness training. The research team is currently conducting further, more extensive, research on mindfulness with primary-school children, focusing on changes in brain markers of attention and emotion regulation.

Reference:

Vickery, C. & Dorjee, D. (2015), 'Mindfulness Training in Primary Schools Decreases Negative Affect and Increases Meta-cognition in Children', *Frontiers in Educational Psychology*.

Acknowledgements

You know how at the end of some books there are pages and pages of acknowledgements to friends, co-workers, family members, researchers, Nobel Prize-winners, professors and mentors? Well, I didn't have any of those. I wrote this book alone. No one helped me write it.

I would have liked to pay homage, like other authors, saying things like, 'I'd like to thank my inspiration and visionary, friend and neighbour Betty F. Soupalski for holding my hand and my head over the sink during my nights of darkness; always there to bring over muffins when I couldn't go on'; 'Al Kackner (now deceased) for his undying devotion and bravery. Even during his last few breaths, while his heart monitor was flat-lining, he still managed to correct my punctuation'; 'I want to thank with deepest humility my hundreds of supporters who tweeted me. I am forever awed by your relentless love. I couldn't have finished this without you'; or 'I'm grateful to Aristotle and Socrates, for passing me their wisdom; allowing me to carry the flame. Thank you both.'

But, as I said before, I was alone when I wrote this, except for my friend and editor, Joanna Bowen, who made this book comprehensible and worked slavishly all hours, and my family, who somehow managed to tolerate me during my mood swings.

There was also my publisher, Venetia Butterfield from

Acknowledgements

Penguin, and my agent, Caroline Michel, who made this book happen.

There were those who made sure the neuroscience, though simplified, still had validity. So I would like to thank Dr Dusana Dorjee, cognitive neuroscientist leading research at the Centre for Mindfulness Research and Practice, for looking into my brain; Jody Mardula, the ex-director of the Centre for Mindfulness Research and Practice; Professor Oliver Turnbull, Pro-vice Chancellor (Teaching and Learning) at Bangor University; Andrew Dellis, postdoctoral Fellow at the Research Unit in Behavioural Economics and Neuroeconomics at the University of Cape Town; Dr Willem Kuyken, Director of the Oxford Mindfulness Centre; Paul Mullins, who did the MRI scan on me; Chris Cullen, co-founder of the Mindfulness in Schools project; Mark Williams, Professor of Clinical Psychology and Wellcome Principal Research Fellow at the University of Oxford, who, with colleagues John D. Teasdale and Zindel Segal, developed Mindfulness-based Cognitive Therapy; and Sharon Grace Hadley, the Centre Manager for the Centre for Mindfulness Research and Practice, for setting up everything at Bangor University.

I would also like to thank the many brilliant authors whose works I've translated into my own words. They are:

Sharon Begley: *Train Your Mind, Change Your Brain: How a New Science Reveals Our Extraordinary Potential to Transform Ourselves*

Sarah-Jayne Blakemore and Uta Frith: *The Learning Brain: Lessons for Education*

Vidyamala Burch and Danny Penman: *Mindfulness for Health: A Practical Guide to Relieving Pain, Reducing Stress and Restoring Wellbeing*

Acknowledgements

Rebecca Crane: *Mindfulness-based Cognitive Therapy: Distinctive Features*

Joe Dispenza: *Evolve Your Brain: The Science of Changing Your Mind*

Janey Downshire and Naella Grew: *Teenagers Translated: How to Raise Happy Teens*

David Eagleman: *The Brain: The Story of You*

Sue Gerhardt: *Why Love Matters*

Paul Gilbert: *The Compassionate Mind: A New Approach to Life's Challenges*

Daniel Goleman: *Focus: The Hidden Driver of Excellence*

Rick Hanson: *Buddha's Brain*

Steven Johnson: *Mind Wide Open: Your Brain and the Neuroscience of Everyday Life*

Jon Kabat-Zinn: *Full Catastrophe Living: How to Cope with Stress, Pain and Illness Using Mindfulness Meditation*

Daniel J. Levitin: *The Organized Mind: Thinking Straight in the Age of Information Overload*

Matthew D. Lieberman: *Social: Why Our Brains are Wired to Connect*

Bruce H. Lipton: *The Biology of Belief: Unleashing the Power of Consciousness, Matter and Miracles*

Jack Kornfield: *A Path with Heart*

Dr Shanida Nataraja: *The Blissful Brain: Neuroscience and Proof of the Power of Meditation*

Robert M. Sapolsky: *Why Zebras Don't Get Ulcers*

Daniel J. Siegel: *Brainstorm: The Power and Purpose of the Teenage Brain*

Daniel Siegel: *Mindsight: The New Science of Personal Transformation*

Daniel J. Siegel and Mary Hartzell: *Parenting from the Inside Out: How a Deeper Self-understanding Can Help You Raise Children Who Thrive*

Acknowledgements

Eline Snel: *Sitting Still like a Frog*

Chade-Meng Tan: *Search Inside Yourself* (series)

Paul Tough: *How Children Succeed*

Mark Williams and Danny Penman: *Mindfulness: A Practical Guide to Finding Peace in a Frantic World*

Mark Williams, John Teasdale, Zindel Segal and Jon Kabat-Zinn: *The Mindful Way through Depression: Freeing Yourself from Chronic Unhappiness*

And I can't forget the many authors of the scientific research papers I borrowed information from:

Dr Elena Antonova, 'Neuroscience of Empathy and Compassion', Institute of Psychiatry

J. A. Brefczynski-Lewis, A. Lutz, H. S. Schaefer, D. B. Levinson and R. J. Davidson: 'Neural Correlates of Attentional Expertise in Long-term Meditation Practitioners' (2007)

Kirk Warren Brown, Richard M. Ryan and J. David Creswell: 'Mindfulness: Theoretical Foundations and Evidence for Its Salutary Effects' (2010)

Kalina Christoff, Alan M. Gordon, Jonathan Smallwood, Rachelle Smith and Jonathan W. Schooler: 'Experience Sampling during fMRI Reveals Default Network and Executive System Contributions to Mind Wandering' (2009)

Richard J. Davidson: 'Well-being and Affective Style: Neural Substrates and Biobehavioural Correlates' (2004)

Richard J. Davidson and Antoine Lutz: 'Buddha's Brain, Neuroplasticity and Meditation' (2008)

Dr Dusana Dorjee: *Mind, Brain and the Path to Happiness: A Guide to Buddhist Mind Training and the Neuroscience of Meditation* (2013)

Norman A. S. Farb, Zindel V. Segal, Helen Mayberg, Jim Bean, Deborah McKeon, Zainab Fatima and Adam K.

Acknowledgements

Anderson: 'Attending to the Present: Mindfulness Meditation Reveals Distinct Neural Modes of Self-reference' (2007)

Michael D. Fox, Abraham Z. Snyder, Justin L. Vincent, Maurizio Corbetta, David C. Van Essen and Marcus E. Raichle: 'The Human Brain is Intrinsically Organized into Dynamic, Anti-correlated Functional Networks' (2005)

Jonathan P. Godbout and Ronald Glaser: 'Stress-induced Immune Deregulation: Implications for Wound Healing, Infectious Disease and Cancer' (2006)

Britta K. Hölzel, Sara W. Lazar, Tim Gard, Zev Schuman-Olivier, David R. Vago and Ulrich Ott: 'How Does Mindfulness Meditation Work: Perspectives on Psychological Science' (2011)

Troels W. Kjaer, Camilla Bertelsen, Paola Piccini, David Brooks, Jørgen Alving and Hans C. Lou: 'Increased Dopamine Tone during Meditation-induced Change of Consciousness' (2002)

Antoine Lutz, Julie Brefczynski-Lewis, Tom Johnstone, Richard J. Davidson: 'Regulation of the Neural Circuitry of Emotion by Compassion Meditation: Effects of Meditation Expertise' (2008)

Antoine Lutz, Lawrence L. Greischar, Nancy B. Rawlings, Matthieu Ricard and Richard J. Davidson: 'Long-term Meditators Self-induce High-amplitude Gamma Synchrony during Mental Practice' (2004)

Antoine Lutz, Heleen A. Slagter, John D. Dunne and Richard J. Davidson: 'Attention Regulation and Monitoring in Meditation: Cognitive-emotional Interactions' (2011)

J. Mark, G. Williams, John D. Teasdale, Judith M. Soulsby, Zindel V. Segal, Valerie A. Ridgeway and Mark A. Lau: 'Prevention of Relapse/Recurrence in Major Depression by Mindfulness-based Cognitive Therapy' (2000)

Acknowledgements

Malia F. Mason, Michel I. Norton, John D. Van Horn, Daniel M. Wegner, Scott T. Grafton, C. Neil Macrae: 'Wandering Minds: The Default Network and Stimulus-independent Thought' (2007)

Katie A. McLaughlin and Susan Nolen-Hoeksema: 'Rumination as a Transdiagnostic Factor in Depression and Anxiety' (2010)

K. L. Mills, F. Lalonde, L. S. Clasen, J. N. Giedd and S. J. Blakemore: 'Developmental Changes in the Structure of the Social Brain in Late Childhood and Adolescence' (2014)

Jaak Panksepp and Douglas Watt: 'What is Basic about Basic Emotions? Lasting Lessons from Affective Neuroscience' (2011)

Katya Rubia: 'The Neurobiology of Meditation and Its Clinical Effectiveness in Psychiatric Disorders' (2009)

Tania Singer, Ben Seymour, John O. Doherty, Holger Kaube, Raymond J. Dolan and Chris Frith: 'Empathy for Pain Involves the Affective but not Sensory Components of Pain' (2004)

Heleen A. Slagter, Richard J. Davidson and Antoine Lutz: 'Mental Training as a Tool in the Neuroscientific Study of Brain and Cognitive Plasticity: Frontiers in Human Neuroscience' (2011)

Jonathan Smallwood and Jonathan W. Schooler: 'The Restless Mind' (2006)

Jonathan Smallwood, Daniel J. Fishman and Jonathan W. Schooler: 'Counting the Cost of an Absent Mind: Mind Wandering as an Under-recognized Influence on Educational Performance' (2007)

Jonathan Smallwood, Merrill McSpadden and Jonathan W. Schooler: 'The Lights are on but No One's Home:

Acknowledgements

Meta-awareness and the Decoupling of Attention When the Mind Wanders' (2007)

Yi-Yuan Tang, Britta K. Hölzel and Michael I. Posner: 'The Neuroscience of Mindfulness Meditation' (2015)

Edward R. Watkins: 'Constructive and Unconstructive Repetitive Thought' (2008)

And many others who shall remain nameless, because I haven't mentioned them, but, hopefully, they know who they are, and I thank them.

Index

Index

Index

Index

Index

Index

Index

He just wanted a decent book to read ...

Not too much to ask, is it? It was in 1935 when Allen Lane, Managing
Director of Bodley Head Publishers, stood on a platform at Exeter railway
station looking for something good to read on his journey back to London.
His choice was limited to popular magazines and poor-quality paperbacks –
the same choice faced every day by the vast majority of readers, few of
whom could afford hardbacks. Lane's disappointment and subsequent anger
at the range of books generally available led him to found a company – and
change the world.

'We believed in the existence in this country of a vast reading public for intelligent
books at a low price, and staked everything on it'
Sir Allen Lane, 1902–1970, founder of Penguin Books

The quality paperback had arrived – and not just in bookshops. Lane was
adamant that his Penguins should appear in chain stores and tobacconists,
and should cost no more than a packet of cigarettes.

Reading habits (and cigarette prices) have changed since 1935, but
Penguin still believes in publishing the best books for everybody to
enjoy. We still believe that good design costs no more than bad design,
and we still believe that quality books published passionately and responsibly
make the world a better place.

So wherever you see the little bird – whether it's on a piece of
prize-winning literary fiction or a celebrity autobiography, political tour
de force or historical masterpiece, a serial-killer thriller, reference book,
world classic or a piece of pure escapism – you can bet that it represents
the very best that the genre has to offer.

Whatever you like to read – trust Penguin.

read more
www.penguin.co.uk